The

NASHVILLE
GUIDE

Experience Local

no. 1

Publisher: Paul McGahren

Editorial Director: Matthew Teague

Editor: Kerri Grzybicki

Layout and Design: Abby Reuther and Lindsay Hess

Photography and Writing: As noted throughout

Spring House Press
P.O. Box 239
Whites Creek, TN 37189

ISBN: 978-1-940611-55-6

Library of Congress Control Number: 2016963212

Printed in the United States of America

10 9 8 7 6 5 4 3 2

To learn more about Spring House Press books, or to find a retailer near you, email info@springhousepress.com or visit us at www.springhousepress.com.

The

NASHVILLE
GUIDE

This is a community collaboration, with the purpose of providing you with an insider's guide to experiencing the best Nashville has to offer. With each of the 10 contributing writers relating their own personal and relevant descriptions, you're getting a guided tour of Nashville's many restaurants, retailers, and must-visit sites from a local perspective. From popular coffee shops to dive bars to small local shops, this handy guide won't disappoint. Be sure to take it along as you explore and experience the thriving Nashville scene like a local.

A portion of our sales will go back to the community, benefiting non-profits and people in need. Follow our journey on Instagram at *@TheNashvilleGuide* and *thenashvilleguide.com*.

CONTENTS

EAT + DRINK

EAT + DRINK *continued*

SHOP

ADVENTURE + ENTERTAINMENT

HEALTH + BEAUTY

EAT + DRINK

juice + smoothies

FRANKLIN JUICE COMPANY

OVERVIEW: This cold-pressed juice joint serves other healthy eats, including specialty coffee, smoothies, and acai, pitaya, or mango bowls.

COST: $$

ADDRESS: 2301 12th Ave S

NEIGHBORHOOD: 12 South

HOURS: Every day, 7am – 7pm

PHONE: 1.615.600.4558

WEBSITE: franklinjuice.com

INSTAGRAM: @franklinjuice

ATMOSPHERE: Its clean white color palette makes the small space inviting and cozy. Their juice masters are welcoming and friendly, making you feel right at home.

HIGHLIGHTS: Personally, I'm a fresh juice lover, so in my opinion you can't ever go wrong with any type of fresh juice—but they set themselves apart by using local, organic fruits and vegetables. Their juices are also non-HPP (high-pressure processed), which is a huge plus.

INSIDER TIPS: They have four different juice cleanses you can order online. Try the Big Island acai bowl—it's to die for. If you're an avocado lover, try the Avo smoothie—you can thank me later.

PHOTOS (LEFT TO RIGHT): Lauren Crawford (@laurenallyson) and Mary Kacy, A. (@marykacyadz)

WRITER: Abby Reuther (@abby.reuther)

I LOVE JUICE BAR

OVERVIEW:
What do you do when it's halfway through the year and you haven't started your New Year's resolution for #CleanEating? Insert: Juice Bar.

Juices, smoothies, power shots, and essential oils, made fresh on the spot with 100% local, organic whole fruits and vegetables. Each well-prepared snack provides a mouthwatering experience you'll want to keep going back for.

COST: $$

ADDRESS: 1120 4th Ave N
For their other locations, please visit the website.

NEIGHBORHOOD: Germantown

HOURS: Mon – Fri, 7am – 5:30pm
Sat, 8:30am – 4:30pm
Sun, 11am – 4pm

WEBSITE: ilovejuicebar.com

INSTAGRAM: @ilovejuicebar

COMMUNITY FAVORITE:
Bunny Love Juice
Kale & Quinoa Salad

PHOTOS (LEFT TO RIGHT):
Holly Darnell (@hollywood_25)
Christine Li (@xinerz)
Sarah Patton (@sarahcharlottepatton)
Mallory Hobson (@malhobz)

WRITER:
Aubrey Hine (@aubreyhine)

ATMOSPHERE:

When you walk into any of the Nashville-hosted locations, you are quickly welcomed by one of the juice masters. Each bar's character captures a little part of Nashville's rustic style, featuring the primitive elements of exposed brick, natural wood detail, and metal high-tops.

Their Germantown location has a great covered patio with seating and games like ping pong, and corn hole!

HIGHLIGHTS:

The Juice Bar's fresh juices, made on the spot, are the most favored items on the menu. Ginger Greens (ginger/apple/kale/spinach/cucumber/parsley/lemon) has been my go-to order for months. However, I've recently fallen in love with their root juice, Bunny Love (carrot/apple/ginger/lemon). Starting my day with a fresh juice keeps me feeling revitalized, especially after an intense workout when my body needs replenishing. Their juices help to boost and increase your immune system and total energy level while assisting in overall weight loss.

INSIDER TIPS:

Sign up for their text message alerts and you'll receive notifications for daily deals: 15% off juice cleanses, 50% off Monster Shots, Free Green add-on, and a size upgrade. Check in with easy entry of your phone number on their tablet every time you make a purchase and you'll receive a large juice on your 10th visit! Download The Juice Bar's ToGo App and order ahead of time from your nearest Juice Bar.

coffee + breakfast + brunch

STEADFAST COFFEE

OVERVIEW: Steadfast Coffee serves coffee, lunch, and dinner in the heart of Germantown. Famous for their Matchless Coffee Soda—it's a must try!

COST: $$

ADDRESS: 603 Taylor St

NEIGHBORHOOD: Germantown

HOURS: Mon - Fri, 7am - 7pm
Sat - Sun, 8am - 7pm

PHONE: 1.615.891.7424

WEBSITE: steadfast.coffee

INSTAGRAM: @steadfastcoffee

ATMOSPHERE: You'll find a diverse crowd here—students, bloggers, musicians, entrepreneurs, etc.—enjoying the natural light, metal bar stools, outdoor seating, and staff in jean aprons.

HIGHLIGHTS: You can literally go here for coffee in the morning and stay for brunch, lunch, and dinner—it's that good. Oh, and they have a great cocktail and beer selection too.

INSIDER TIPS: Order the Side Sausage, the Roasted Vegetable Salad, and a Matchless Coffee Soda. Need a little pick-me-up? Ask for the Wolfpack (Matchless Coffee Soda, Ramazzotti, and mint).

PHOTOS (LEFT TO RIGHT):
Kelsey Sykes (@oldtimefeeling)
and Kathleen Clipper (@thenewgirlinnashville)

WRITER:
Kate Moore (@moore_kate)

DOZEN BAKERY

OVERVIEW:
This bright and minimal space features baked goods in the French tradition, fresh breads, breakfast, and lunch. Dozen's creativity in flavor profiles for salads and sandwiches are unmatched and change with the seasons. Indulge in your lunch here with a peek at the largest oven you've even seen!

COST: $$

ADDRESS: 516 Hagan St #103

NEIGHBORHOOD: Wedgewood Houston

HOURS: Mon – Sat, 7am – 6pm
Sun, 9am – 3pm

PHONE: 1.615.712.8150

WEBSITE: dozen-nashville.com

INSTAGRAM: @dozenbakerynashville

COMMUNITY FAVORITE:
Try the Blueberry Muffins, Benton's Bacon Sandwich, and the Farro Salad.

PHOTOS (LEFT TO RIGHT):
Emily Lunstroth (@emilylunstroth)
Maggie Eckford (@maggieeckford)
Rachel V. Miller (@rvmillz)
Olivia L. (@TheNashvilleKid)

WRITER:
Alex Tapper (@fantasticmrtapp)

ATMOSPHERE:

You'll find a clean, well-lit corner space of an old truck repair station, featuring high ceilings, minimal design, and a garage door that opens onto an umbrella-covered patio. The seasonal menu is written, by hand, on a long sheet of butcher paper behind the counter. Fresh pies are in the cooler, and a glorious spread of baked goods is neatly labeled and lined up behind the glass.

HIGHLIGHTS:

They bake all of the bread in-house. The seasonal menu changes just often enough to keep up with what's fresh, so you'll often find something new—and that includes the baked goods. But there will always be the classic French staples too: the perfect croissant, lemon madeleines, kouign-amann, and galettes. Oh, and the pies! Lemon lavender is my favorite, but you'll also find chocolate peanut butter, peach, and others, depending on the season. The most unique things on the menu are the "salads," which are in quotes because only 1 out of 5 are usually leafy. These hearty sides utilize unique flavor combinations like roasted broccoli and oranges, buckwheat noodles with summer peaches and burrata, or farro with pickled parsnips and Castelvetrano olives. These fresh, unique flavor profiles steal the show.

INSIDER TIPS:

Lunch is their specialty, offering a cost effective salad and sandwich combo at $9. On Fridays only, you can pick up challah, with poppy seeds or traditional. It's so good you just have to tear at it with your hands!

EDGEHILL CAFE

OVERVIEW: Edgehill Cafe features wide variety of delicious coffee, breakfast, brunch, and lunch options in a cozy comfortable space.

COST: $$

ADDRESS: 1201 Villa Pl

NEIGHBORHOOD: Edgehill Village

HOURS: Mon - Sat, 7am - 10pm
Sun, 9am - 4pm

PHONE: 1.615.942.5717

WEBSITE: edgehillcafe.com

INSTAGRAM: @edgehillcafe

ATMOSPHERE: This cafe is full of local entrepreneurs and musicians who are in for a cup of coffee or a hot breakfast. The cozy atmosphere is equally perfect for meetings and quiet working. The large windows provide the most amazing natural light in this spot where everybody knows your name and is super friendly.

HIGHLIGHTS: The Always Fall Somewhere is an absolute must, and accompanied by Red Velvet Pancakes, you cannot go wrong.

INSIDER TIPS: Show up first thing in the morning to miss the crowd and enjoy the morning light. Hit them up for brunch on Saturdays and Sundays featuring mimosas, coffee, and eggs!

PHOTOS (LEFT TO RIGHT):
Kris D'Amico (@damicophoto) and Abby Palmer (@abbyaleece)

WRITER: Kate Moore (@moore_kate)

THREE BROTHERS COFFEE

OVERVIEW: This coffee shop serves coffee, prepared snacks, sandwiches, and pastries, all from local roasters and bakeries.

COST: $

ADDRESS: 2813 West End Ave

NEIGHBORHOOD: West End

HOURS: Mon – Fri, 6am – 7pm
Sat – Sun, 8am – 7pm

PHONE: 1.615.835.2166

WEBSITE: threebroscoffee.com

INSTAGRAM: @threebrotherscoffee

ATMOSPHERE: This bright, clean space has individual and community tables, as well as bar-style seating. Its a great place to study, work, or catch up with friends.

HIGHLIGHTS: Unlike many Nashville coffee shops, it is not yet overcrowded, so it's a reliable place to camp out for a morning or afternoon. And on nice days when the garage doors are open, the bar seats turn into a great open-air spot to people-watch.

INSIDER TIPS: There is free parking in the back, but this can fill up fast. Be prepared to find metered or street parking.

PHOTOS (LEFT TO RIGHT):
Erin Vondohlen (@imrunnin_erins)
Rachel Li (@lovefrom_rachel)

WRITER: Kristen Shoates (@kristennicole86)

FIVE DAUGHTERS BAKERY

OVERVIEW:
Five Daughters specializes in the highly sought-after cronut, a combination of a croissant and a donut. Nestled among the long line of specialty shops in 12 South, it's exactly what you'd expect from a sweet family-run and -operated business.

COST: $$

ADDRESS: 1110 Caruthers Ave

NEIGHBORHOOD: 12 South

HOURS: Mon – Fri, 7am – 10pm (or 'til sold out)
Sat – Sun, 9am – 4pm (or 'til sold out)

PHONE: 1.615.490.6554

WEBSITE: fivedaughtersbakery.com

INSTAGRAM: @five_daughters_bakery

COMMUNITY FAVORITE:
There are so many good flavors: Milk Chocolate Sea Salt, Vanilla Cream, and Maple…and Blueberry Lemon…probably the Samoa too. I can't stop!

PHOTOS (LEFT TO RIGHT):
Bay Brooks (@baybrooksmusic)
Kathleen Clipper (@thenewgirlinnashville)
Victoria Morris (@vmorris41)
Lauren Pendleton (@laurenmpendleton)

WRITER:
Aubrey Hine (@aubreyhine)

ATMOSPHERE:

The shop's interior encompasses both a vintage and modern flair, with weathered floors, sleek white subway tile, charming display items, lovable photos of the owners' five daughters (wink, wink), and a large neon FIVE DAUGHTERS BAKERY sign to tie it all together. Flow from room to room in the small, yet inviting space until you reach the display case of cronuts to make your final decision.

HIGHLIGHTS:

The delicious selection of 100-layer cronuts is one for the books—and definitely worth the wait. What makes these confections so desirable is what's on the inside. Every cronut is handmade daily from fresh, locally sourced ingredients. The puffed cream, glazes, and toppings are combined and layered without any artificial colors, preservatives, or flavors. What is done in love is done well (as Vincent van Gogh once said). You can see and taste the love that is put into every single batch, and these are by far some of the best local treats in Nashville.

To top it off, the bakery also offers "Paleo Crushers" for those who desire a gluten-, dairy-, and sugar-free option!

INSIDER TIPS:

Don't just get one, get a dozen at least! Go during the week or early on the weekend as the line can get a little long during peak hours. There's also a donut cam on their website for a sneak peak of the sugar-coated adventure you're about to embark on.

JUST LOVE COFFEE

OVERVIEW: This is a coffee shop serving a full breakfast, lunch, and dinner menu. Their coffee is guaranteed fresh, and is hand-roasted at their roasting facility in Murfeesboro, Tennessee.

COST: $

ADDRESS: 1528 Demonbreun St

NEIGHBORHOOD: Demonbreun Hill

HOURS: Every day, 7am - 7 pm

PHONE: 1.615.891.2708

WEBSITE: justlovecoffee.com

INSTAGRAM: @justlovemusicrow

ATMOSPHERE: There's ample seating and a large bar where you can sit and watch the baristas as they work.

HIGHLIGHTS: They have salads, wraps, and other entrees. You can't forget the Nitro Coffee–cold-brewed coffee infused with nitrogen.

The owners truly believe in "people before profit" and I could give them a big hug for that. They give a large portion of their profits to worthy causes.

INSIDER TIPS: Parking is limited. There are a couple paid lots around the area that usually offer the first hour free or for a low rate.

PHOTOS (LEFT TO RIGHT):
Dan Voris (@DCVRS)
Ghada, Bawajeeh (@ghadawb)

WRITER: Abby Reuther (@abby.reuther)

YEAST NASHVILLE

OVERVIEW: Everything good rises in the East! They specialize in Czech- and Texas-style kolaches—a sweet pastry stuffed with meat or fruit—but also feature a thoughtful menu with rotating daily specials and espresso concoctions.

COST: $

ADDRESS: 805 Woodland St #300

NEIGHBORHOOD: East Nashville

HOURS: Every day, 7am – 1pm

PHONE: 1.615.678.4592

WEBSITE: yeastnashville.com

INSTAGRAM: @yeastnashville

ATMOSPHERE: The sweet smell of fresh kolaches floods through the door as soon as you walk in. There is an open seating area that over looks the bakery kitchen, so you can get a first-hand look at their master craft. This is a no-frills, quality breakfast spot for locals.

HIGHLIGHTS: Tex-Czech kolaches come in sweet or savory varieties, and pair nicely with a latte or coffee. Don't overlook the breakfast tacos or frittata.

INSIDER TIPS: Pick up breakfast on-the-go or hang around for some WiFi time. Either way, get there early if you want the kolache o' the day!

PHOTOS (LEFT TO RIGHT):
Hadley Kennary (@hadleykennary)
Holly Darnell (@hollywood_25)

WRITER: Alex Tapper (@fantasticmrtapp)

BARISTA PARLOR

OVERVIEW:
Barista Parlor is a serious
East Nashville coffee shop with delicious
food, strong coffee, thoughtful design, and
cool kids.

COST: $$

ADDRESS: 519 Gallatin Ave
*For their other locations, please visit
the website.*

NEIGHBORHOOD: East Nashville

HOURS: Mon – Fri, 7am – 8pm
Sat – Sun, 8am – 8pm

PHONE: 1.615.712.9766

WEBSITE: baristaparlor.com

INSTAGRAM: @baristaparlor

COMMUNITY FAVORITE:
Cold Brew
Vanilla Bourbon
Biscuits
Breakfast Burrito
Habanero Salt Chocolate
...basically everything on the menu!

PHOTOS (LEFT TO RIGHT):
Anna Greenberg (@annabridget)
Savannah Ruth Wiggins (@theblondewig)
Sarah Easterling (@sarahiu10)
Jillian Firns (@jillianskrillian)

WRITER:
Allison Holley (@appleandoaknash)

ATMOSPHERE:
Located in a rehabbed auto repair shop, with giant garage doors and vintage motorcycles on display, this spot's decor is meticulous and definitely photo-worthy. They also have a small partially covered seating area in front of the coffee shop.

HIGHLIGHTS:
The coffee is strong: drink accordingly. The pour-over and the cold brew have been known to cause the jitters. While coffee is the star, the food is also excellent. You can't go wrong on the food menu.

They sell their own Barista Parlor Coffee Boxes so you can enjoy their coffee at home. They also sell a variety of coffee cups, glasses, and even growlers.

INSIDER TIPS:
On the weekends, expect to wait in line and then expect to wait for your order, but it's worth the wait. You can find a place to sit after you order, so it all works out, and there's no need to send someone to hold a place. Keep calm—coffee magic is in the works.

This isn't a diner; some knowledge of coffee is helpful. Try not to ask for cream, sugar, or flavor shots—trust me, you won't need any of it.

Oh, and that small human they hand you is your table marker (you'll understand soon).

UGLY MUGS COFFEE & TEA

OVERVIEW: This is a coffee shop serving local roasted coffee, breakfast, lunch, and dessert.

COST: $

ADDRESS: 1886 Eastland Ave

NEIGHBORHOOD: East Nashville

HOURS: Mon – Fri, 6am – 10pm
Sat – Sun, 7am – 10pm

PHONE: 1.615.915.0675

WEBSITE: uglymugsnashville.com

INSTAGRAM: @uglymugs

ATMOSPHERE: Ugly Mugs has everything you'd want in a coffee shop: artwork from local artists; regular live, local music; comfy couches; and the aroma of coffee. It's the perfect place to work, meet with friends, or enjoy a good cup of coffee and eats.

HIGHLIGHTS: They're great supporters of local. Their coffee is roasted in East Nashville by Drew's Brews, and sweets hail from Sweet 16th, Dozen Bakery, Bagel Face Bakery, and more.

INSIDER TIPS: It's nestled among other restaurants and shops—The Wild Cow, Graze, Welcome Home shop, Jeni's Splendid Ice Creams, and many more.

PHOTOS (LEFT TO RIGHT):
Greer M. (@greerr.io) and Honey Cox (@peechyhoney)

WRITER:
Kelley Griggs (@kelleyboothe)

THE JAM COFFEE HOUSE

OVERVIEW: The Jam Coffee House is a family-owned, '50s-inspired coffee house. I can't say it better than they do: "There are two things we firmly believe in: that *delicious* and *nutritious* should be in the same sentence, and that we all need a place to belong."

COST: $$

ADDRESS: 1210 Wedgewood Ave

NEIGHBORHOOD: Edgehill Village

HOURS: Mon – Fri, 7am – 3pm
Sat – Sun, 9am – 3pm

PHONE: 1.615.823.3292

WEBSITE: thejamcoffeehouse.com

INSTAGRAM: @thejamnashville

ATMOSPHERE: You walk into a little strip mall behind what used to be a drive-through gas station and into this adorable little coffee oasis.

HIGHLIGHTS: They have about five things on their food menu and they're all perfect. I try a new coffee or tea treat every time I go—it never gets old!

INSIDER TIPS: Get the Good Morning Tacos—sprouted corn tortillas, local scrambled eggs, raw cheddar cheese, ripe avocado, and their homemade taco sauce.

PHOTOS (LEFT TO RIGHT):
Jessica Soccorsi (@jess_soccorsi) and Kerri Ruffer (@kerrinicoler)

WRITER:
Kate Moore (@moore_kate)

PANCAKE PANTRY

OVERVIEW:
The name probably says it all, but they're known for "Nashville's Best Pancakes." They've been a Nashville staple since 1961, and the old '60s charm still remains intact.

If you've ever driven by, you'll also probably know them for the long line that wraps around the corner. Every day, people patiently wait to claim a table and get their hands on the delicious pancakes.

COST: $

ADDRESS: 1796 21st Ave S

NEIGHBORHOOD: Hillsboro Village

HOURS: Mon - Fri, 6am - 3pm
Sat - Sun, 6am - 4pm

PHONE: 1.615.383.9333

WEBSITE: thepancakepantry.com

INSTAGRAM: @thepancakepantry

COMMUNITY FAVORITE:
The pancakes (obviously): Original buttermilk, blueberry, pecan, Georgia peach—the list goes on and on, and you really can't go wrong.

PHOTOS (LEFT TO RIGHT):
Emilie Sobel (@emiliesobel)
Jaclyn Kreft (@jaclynkreft)
Justine Pepe (@lovejpep)
Abby Reuther (@abby.reuther)

WRITER:
Sarah Patton (@sarahcharlottepatton)

ATMOSPHERE:

The brick building is unassuming and the inside is a humble space full of booths and tables. There's been no contemporary update, but that's what makes the space authentic. There's no need to impress with the decor because the food is delicious.

HIGHLIGHTS:

The owner often gets asked about their pancake and waffle ingredients. They use specialty flours from East Tennessee and make their batter and syrups fresh each day from their family-secret recipes. These might be some of Nashville's best-kept secrets, if you ask me.

My go-to order is the Sausage and Cheese Omelet. I know, you're probably wondering why I order eggs at the pancake headquarters, but the crumpled sausage is to die for. Not to mention, most menu items that aren't specialty pancakes come with three buttermilk pancakes on the side—a win-win for sure!

INSIDER TIPS:

It's a celebrity spotting site, so be on the lookout—you never know who you'll see scarfing down those delicious pancakes.

No reservations are accepted. It's a first-come, first-served restaurant. Be prepared to wait in line and hold your spot, but it's worth the long wait. Dress appropriately for the weather to wait in line too.

THE PFUNKY GRIDDLE

OVERVIEW: This is a pancake cafe where each table is topped with its own grill, making it an interactive experience for guests and fun for all!

Not a pancake lover or don't want to cook your own food? They have a wide variety of soups, salads, and sandwiches.

COST: $

ADDRESS: 2800 Bransford Ave

NEIGHBORHOOD: Berry Hill

HOURS: Tues – Thur, 8am – 2pm
Sat – Sun, 7am – 3pm

PHONE: 1.615.298.2088

WEBSITE: thepfunkygriddle.com

INSTAGRAM: @pfunkygriddle1

ATMOSPHERE: It's homey and laid back, just like grandma's kitchen! No need to get dressed up; casual is best.

HIGHLIGHTS: You get to cook your own pancakes with a variety of toppings, making them just as you like. They have gluten-free pancake batter for all my gluten-conscious friends.

INSIDER TIPS: There's usually a long wait for breakfast on the weekends, so get there early.

PHOTOS (LEFT TO RIGHT):
Jennifer & Dean Tutor (@2HappyHUngryNomads)
Mikayla Willis (@mikdanwillis)

WRITER: Abby Reuther (@abby.reuther)

SKY BLUE CAFE

OVERVIEW: Sky Blue Cafe is a neighborhood diner serving local coffee, baked goods, breakfast specialties, and lunch in a cozy, colorful corner restaurant.

COST: $

ADDRESS: 700 Fatherland St

NEIGHBORHOOD: East Nashville

HOURS: Every day, 7am – 4pm

PHONE: 1.615.770.7097

WEBSITE: skybluecoffee.com

INSTAGRAM: @skybluecafe

ATMOSPHERE: Located in the heart of Edgefield's Historic District in East Nashville, Sky Blue Cafe is an eclectic daily stop for neighbors and off-the-beaten-path visitors.

HIGHLIGHTS: The lattes are often made to order, but the creme-de-la-creme at Sky Blue is the French toast. Ask for Nutella for a morning treat.

INSIDER TIPS: Take a seat near the windows or outside on the patio for an experience not complete without a few quick games of lightning-round Trivial Pursuit.

Be prepared to wait for a table on the weekends or, better yet, get there early to hopefully avoid the wait altogether.

PHOTOS (LEFT TO RIGHT):
Liz Burley (@lizburleyphoto)
Marilyn Lauterbach (@NashvilleFoodAuthority)

WRITER: Kelley Griggs (@kelleyboothe)

PROPER BAGEL

OVERVIEW:
Proper Bagel is a NY-style bagel shop and market specializing in breakfast and lunch that serves a variety of housemade bagels, sandwiches, salads, soups, and pastries.

COST: $$

ADDRESS: 2011 Belmont Blvd

NEIGHBORHOOD: Belmont Blvd

HOURS: Mon – Fri, 7:30am – 4pm
Sat – Sun, 8am – 4pm

PHONE: 1.615.928.7276

WEBSITE: properbagel.com

INSTAGRAM: @properbagel

COMMUNITY FAVORITE:
Smashed Avocado Toast—fresh smashed avocado, arugula, seared tomato, and pickled radish.

New Yorker Bagel—farm egg, applewood bacon or local sage sausage, white American cheese, and ketchup.

PHOTOS (LEFT TO RIGHT):
Emily Lunstroth (@emilylunstroth)
Madeline Bush (@theageofmadeline)
Nikki R. (@fifthandchurch)
Abigail Olivas (@onehappyplace)

WRITER:
Abby Reuther (@abby.reuther)

ATMOSPHERE:

The interior is a dream. It's hip and edgy—I try to pretend I'm hip enough for it. I wonder if I fool anyone?

It's simple-yet-stunning white and black interior and natural light make you want to take a window seat and stay for hours.

You'll find a good mix of people—Belmont students, corporate professionals, and artsy hipsters.

HIGHLIGHTS:

Proper Bagel partners with the famous local coffee gurus, Barista Parlor, to serve up some delicious coffee.

Their kettle-boiled bagels are made to perfection daily, from scratch, and baked in their stone-lined oven.

Not only do they serve a variety of housemade bagels, but they also have sandwiches, salads, soups, and pastries that will make you lick your lips and come back for more.

Get some goodies from their market to enjoy at home: salads, specialty cream cheeses, seasonal spreads, and a fine selection of smoked fish hand-sliced to order.

INSIDER TIPS:

Be adventurous with your cream cheese spread flavor.

Their white and black interior with mega natural light makes for the perfect Instagram photos. Don't forget to tag @properbagel and @TheNashvilleGuide in your pictures!

BISCUIT LOVE

OVERVIEW: Biscuit Love serves a up true Southern breakfast and lunch made with locally sourced ingredients.

COST: $$

ADDRESS: 316 11th Ave S
For other locations, please visit their website.

NEIGHBORHOOD: The Gulch

HOURS: Every day, 7am – 3pm

PHONE: 1.615.490.9584

WEBSITE: biscuitlove.com

INSTAGRAM: @biscuitlovebrunch

ATMOSPHERE: With exposed, painted brick and soft lighting, this is one of Nashville's most sought-after breakfast spots. Seating is somewhat limited, but as long as you don't mind being friendly with your neighbor, the crowd is worth the experience. Think old-school diner meets Johnny Cash.

HIGHLIGHTS: It's everything you've ever wanted in a breakfast. Savory and sweet (bonuts!) options create a medley of flavor notes that will beg you to return week after week.

INSIDER TIPS: The line of hungry humans will wrap around the building just about every morning. If you're here only for the weekend, plan to get there before it opens. I was lucky (once) to find no line at 8am on a Sunday morning.

PHOTOS (LEFT TO RIGHT):
Allison Cobb (@alkatco) and Dhruvi Patel (@Sprinkleofserendipity)

WRITER: Aubrey Hine (@aubreyhine)

CREMA COFFEE

OVERVIEW: This award-winning specialty coffee roaster serves up coffee, pastries, and snacks.

COST: $$

ADDRESS: 15 Hermitage Ave

NEIGHBORHOOD: Sobro

HOURS: Mon – Fri, 7am – 7pm
Sat, 8am – 6pm, Sun, 9am – 4pm

PHONE: 1.615.255.8311

WEBSITE: crema-coffee.com

INSTAGRAM: @cremacrema

ATMOSPHERE: It's located in the heart of the up-and-coming downtown neighborhood Sobro. This industrial space is the perfect spot to grab a coffee with a friend, work quietly, or eat a tasty snack on their outdoor patio.

HIGHLIGHTS: The owners have traveled the world to find the best coffee farmers and take great pride in the roasting process. The story of how they started the shop is inspiring and I encourage you to read it on their website.

INSIDER TIPS: They offer coffee classes a few times a month to help you achieve great coffee at home—sign up on their website.

Craving their coffee but don't live in Nashville? Good news! You can buy their coffee individually or by subscription on their website.

PHOTOS (LEFT TO RIGHT): Rachel Skaggs (@alifesolovely) Hannah Huffines (@hannahahuffines)

WRITER: Abby Reuther (@abby.reuther)

EAT + DRINK

restaurants

MARCHE ARTISAN FOODS

OVERVIEW: Marche is a popular European-style restaurant that serves seasonal cuisine made from local ingredients. They're open for breakfast, lunch, dinner, and the very popular weekend brunch.

COST: $$

ADDRESS: 1000 Main St

NEIGHBORHOOD: East Nashville

HOURS: Tues – Sat, 8am – 9pm
Sun, 9am – 4pm
Happy hour Tues – Fri, 4pm – 6pm

PHONE: 1.615.262.1111

WEBSITE: marcheartisanfoods.com

INSTAGRAM: @marcheartisanfoods

ATMOSPHERE: Housed in a former telephone switching building, the quaint cafe breathes history.

HIGHLIGHTS: They have a great selection of edible goods from local producers that you can purchase to take home with you. You can find anything from pancake mix to gourmet chocolates to fresh breads, and much more.

INSIDER TIPS: Large windows providing ample natural light make Marche the perfect spot to get jaw-dropping food pictures—hello, gorgeous Instagram posts.

PHOTOS (LEFT TO RIGHT): Mindy Hong (@minstagraams)
Sarah Patton (@sarahcharlottepatton)

WRITER: Abby Reuther (@abby.reuther)

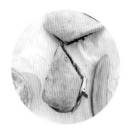

MITCHELL DELICATESSEN

OVERVIEW: This is a deli specializing in fresh artisan sandwiches, with a hot breakfast bar, salad bar, and housemade soup.

COST: $

ADDRESS: 1306 McGavock Pike

NEIGHBORHOOD: East Nashville

HOURS: Mon – Sat, 7am – 10pm
Sun, 8am – 4pm

PHONE: 1.615.262.9862

WEBSITE: mitchelldeli.com

INSTAGRAM: @mitchelldeli

ATMOSPHERE: Order at the counter and take a seat in their casual dinning room. On a nice day, enjoy the large outdoor patio.

HIGHLIGHTS: Most of their meats are cured or smoked in-house; they hand-make their own sausages and roast beef.

Vegetarians and vegans, don't worry: they have amazing local seitan and tofu sandwich options as well.

INSIDER TIPS: Try my favorite, the B.L.T.—it has the tastiest bacon. The outdoor patio is dog friendly.

PHOTOS (LEFT TO RIGHT):
Kim Salter (@designthoughtsSTUDIO)
Kenzie Hruby (@khruby)

WRITER: Abby Reuther (@abby.reuther)

THE CAFE AT THISTLE FARMS

OVERVIEW: A social enterprise run by Thistle Farms, The Cafe at Thistle Farms was built for and by the community. They feature tasty seasonal menus for both breakfast and lunch, and are Nashville's only daily tea service.

COST: $

ADDRESS: 1522 Charlotte Ave

NEIGHBORHOOD: The Nations

HOURS: Mon – Sat, 7am – 3pm

PHONE: 1.615.953.6440

WEBSITE: thecafeatthistlefarms.org

INSTAGRAM: @thecafeatthistlefarms

ATMOSPHERE: The decor is international and made with love. Teacups collected from all over the world hang from the ceiling and represent restoration and the healing power of love. The abundance of space makes it a great place for work or catching up with friends.

HIGHLIGHTS: The cafe is staffed by women with incredible stories. The proceeds support Thistle Farms, a non-profit providing healing and job opportunities for survivors of trafficking, prostitution, addiction, and abuse.

INSIDER TIPS: The cafe can be rented out and offers catering.

PHOTOS (LEFT TO RIGHT):
Britt Reid (@nashvilleveganlookbook)
Helen Bush (@hereandhelen)

WRITER: Kristen Shoates (@kristennicole86)

THE FAMILY WASH

OVERVIEW: The Family Wash is a beloved Nashville-based restaurant, host to a variety of local musicians, community art, Garage Coffee to go, and all-day stacks of buttery blueberry pancakes.

COST: $$

ADDRESS: 626A Main St

NEIGHBORHOOD: East Nashville

HOURS: Mon – Sat, 8am – 1am
Sun, 9am – 3pm

WEBSITE: familywash.com

INSTAGRAM: @familywash

ATMOSPHERE: The grunge-themed, funky style of the restaurant begs the seasoned local to stop by and listen with open eyes, ears, and tastebuds for an authentic experience far from honky-tonk culture.

HIGHLIGHTS: You have to try the Shepherd's Pie; it comes in regular or vegetarian and both versions are delicious.

Don't miss Pies and Pints night every Tuesday, featuring live music and an additional happy hour.

INSIDER TIPS: Don't forget to leave some money for the band and support the local musicians.

PHOTOS (LEFT TO RIGHT):
Ginny Carpenter (@toomuchgin)
Angela Roberts (@spinachtiger)

WRITER: Kelley Griggs (@kelleyboothe)

DESANO PIZZA BAKERY

OVERVIEW: This is a true Neapolitan pizza bakery that uses imported Italian ingredients and hand-kneaded dough, baked in wood-burning ovens.

COST: $$

ADDRESS: 115 16th Ave S

NEIGHBORHOOD: Midtown

HOURS: Mon – Sun, 11am 'til dough runs out

PHONE: 1.615.953.1168

WEBSITE: desanopizza.it

INSTAGRAM: @desanopizza_nashville

ATMOSPHERE: Large, long tables in a spacious dining room create a laid-back atmosphere great for large parties and mingling with others.

HIGHLIGHTS: They offer other Italian specialties such as calzones, salads, gelato (my favorite), and cannolis.

INSIDER TIPS: You're allowed to bring your own wine! Great for take-out and you can even order online—but I still recommend eating there for the experience.

PHOTOS (LEFT TO RIGHT):
Kyler Raymond, Russell (@kyler.raymond)
Aubrey Hine (@aubreyhine)

WRITER: Abby Reuther (@abby.reuther)

43

BUTCHERTOWN HALL

OVERVIEW:
Known for their wood-fire cooking and housemade meats, Butchertown Hall offers a wide range of foods from sausages and short ribs to tacos and sandwiches. It really is all about the meat, and they know how to showcase the flavor well.

COST: $$

ADDRESS: 1416 4th Ave N

NEIGHBORHOOD: Germantown

HOURS: Mon – Thur, 11am – 10pm
Fri, 11am – 11pm
Sat, 10am – 11pm
Sun, 10am – 10pm

PHONE: 1.615.454.3634

WEBSITE: butchertownhall.com

INSTAGRAM: @butchertownhall

COMMUNITY FAVORITE:
Platos de Tacos Buenos (brisket and chicken) on flour tortillas with a side of Street Corn.

PHOTOS (LEFT TO RIGHT):
Erica Vogler (@e_vogue)
Edith Rangel (@edithhrangel)
Carlen Arnold (@hostandtoaststudio)
Edith Rangel (@edithhrangel)

WRITER:
Holly Darnell (@hollywood_25)

ATMOSPHERE:

The decor is breathtaking—it features walls of white stone with open hearths and greenery throughout, and the open kitchen allows diners to watch the chefs prepare and plate the food. It's easy to see why it was voted one of the top 15 most beautiful restaurants in 2015 by Eater U.S.

They also have an amazing outdoor patio with a small covered portion.

HIGHLIGHTS:

Butchertown Hall has an extensive beer list and several companies brew beers specifically for the restaurant. They also have other delicious cocktails available—my all-around favorite is the Paloma.

Basically, any decision you make from the menu is going to be a good one. Their meats are the tastiest. They also make their flour tortillas in-house—I could eat them alone and be a happy gal. They are that good!

INSIDER TIPS:

If you're not feeling too full after dinner, I suggest ordering the Chocolate Chip Cookie Skillet with Maple Bacon Ice Cream.

Butchertown Hall accepts limited reservations on Sunday through Thursday nights, but are walk-in only on the weekends.

Drinks and appetizers can be ordered at the bar while waiting for a table (go for the Guacamole and Queso!) They also offer a delicious brunch on the weekends.

EASTLAND CAFE

OVERVIEW: Eastland Cafe offers a wide variety of exceptional food and fine wine at a great price, as well as daily specials and seasonal dishes.

COST: $$

ADDRESS: 97 Chapel Ave

NEIGHBORHOOD: East Nashville

HOURS: Bar opens at 4:30pm Mon – Sat
Kitchen: Mon – Thur, 5 – 10pm
Fri – Sat, 5 – 11pm

PHONE: 1.615.627.1088

WEBSITE: eastlandcafe.com

INSTAGRAM: @eastlandcafe

ATMOSPHERE: An open, yet intimate dining room with dim romantic lighting is ideal for any occasion: special events, business dinners, casual meals, and date nights.

HIGHLIGHTS: It has a great back patio with streaming lights above—perfect for those mild summer nights. Their staff is exceptional and always makes you feel right at home.

INSIDER TIPS: A large happy hour selection of drinks and tapas is available Monday to Thursday, 4:30 to 6:30pm and Friday to Saturday, 4:30 to 6pm. Personally, I think it's the best happy hour in Nashville and it's super affordable. Make sure to try the Stone Baked Margarita Pizza—it's the best I've had!

PHOTOS (LEFT TO RIGHT):
Blair Beaty (@thehungryleopard)
and Cassandra Neece (@cassandraneece)

WRITER: Abby Reuther (@abby.reuther)

LOVE PEACE & PHO

OVERVIEW: Love Peace & Pho serves traditional Vietnamese food made with fresh ingredients.

COST: $$

ADDRESS: 2112 8th Ave S

NEIGHBORHOOD: 8th Ave

HOURS: Sun - Thur, 11am - 10pm
Fri - Sat, 11am - 11pm

PHONE: 1.615.942.0045

WEBSITE: lovepeaceandpho.com

INSTAGRAM: @lovepeaceandpho

ATMOSPHERE: Mid-century modern meets '70s retro in a funky strip mall—enjoy ambient lighting, wall decals, and period music.

HIGHLIGHTS: For lunch: Banh Mi of your choice (or grilled pork). For a hot day: Vermicelli Rice Noodles (served cold). For the sweet tooth: Vietnamese Coffee with sweetened condensed milk or Boba Tea. For sick days: Pho.

INSIDER TIPS: Pho, pronounced Fuh, is comfort food at the highest level. Sick? Cold? Get it with beef and all of the toppings. Go easy on the heat.

Pictures on the menu help make ordering easier.

PHOTOS (LEFT TO RIGHT):
Anna Leverence (@a_girl_in_dixie)
Abby Reuther (@abby.reuther)

WRITER: Alex Tapper (@fantasticmrtapp)

MAS TACOS POR FAVOR

OVERVIEW:
A food truck turned casual dining restaurant, Mas Tacos Por Favor is a favorite among locals. They feature signature tacos, soups, and sides. It is locally owned and operated by an extraordinary female Nashville native. Featured numerous times on Food Network and in national magazines (for good reason), Mas Tacos is causal, eclectic dining at its best. Food is fresh and prepared to order.

COST: $

ADDRESS: 732 Mcferrin Ave

NEIGHBORHOOD: East Nashville

HOURS: Mon – Fri, 11am – 9pm
Sat, 10am – 9pm

PHONE: 1.615.543.6271

WEBSITE: eatmastacos.com

INSTAGRAM: @mastacos

COMMUNITY FAVORITE:
Try the Pork Taco and Tortilla Soup.

PHOTOS (LEFT TO RIGHT):
Carrie Zinnecker (@biscottiblogger)
Victoria Morris (@vmorris41)
Abby Reuther (@abby.reuther)
Raina Patel (@raina.patel)

WRITER:
Allison Holley (@appleandoaknash)

ATMOSPHERE:

It's a relaxed, casual, and fun atmosphere. You order at the counter and can find seating inside or outside under covered seating.

HIGHLIGHTS:

My personal favorite taco is Cactus & Chorizo, which is heavenly but only available on Thursday.

Tamale Day is Wednesday. They are all hand-rolled and when they run out, that's it. Get there early on Wednesday.

Saturday is brunch, which includes scrambled egg tacos and chilaquiles (if you get there early).

They recently opened their bar. You better try their passion fruit margarita!

INSIDER TIPS:

Okay, I'm going to give it to you straight. I used to work here and I think you can handle this…

It's cash only, tax included, and don't forget to tip! There is an ATM inside if you forget. There will probably be a line, but it typically moves fast and it is so worth it. The menu is above the counter where you order; look at it before you get to the counter. The menu isn't large and everything is yummy. I get two tacos and a soup. No, they don't have chips and salsa. Order the items as they come, especially if it is your first time! Everything is amazing and even if it sounds strange to you, the flavors go so well together. There is no such thing as "a regular taco." When you sit down, don't forget to listen for your name or someone else (me) might get your food.

ROSEPEPPER CANTINA

OVERVIEW: Rosepepper Cantina is home to Nashville's Best Margarita for 11 years and serves homemade tasty Mexican eats.

COST: $$

ADDRESS: 1907 Eastland Ave

NEIGHBORHOOD: East Nashville

HOURS: Mon – Thur, 11am – 2pm,
4pm – 9:30pm
Fri – Sat, 11am – 10:30pm
Sun, 11am – 9:30pm
Hours subject to change depending on season.

PHONE: 1.615.227.4777

WEBSITE: rosepepper.com

INSTAGRAM: @therosepepper

ATMOSPHERE: It's a colorful and quirky restaurant with a fantastic bar and large deck.

HIGHLIGHTS: The Chile Relleno is a roasted poblano chile stuffed with cheese and tempura fried. The Avocado Fries with Buffalo White Cheese Dip are also amazing. Their tequila selection is one of the largest in town.

INSIDER TIPS: For an extra dollar you can upgrade to a top-shelf margarita. Make sure to check out their fun message board out front for a good laugh (see above).

PHOTOS (LEFT TO RIGHT):
Sarah Armendariz (@SA1984)
and Marian Venceslá (@marianvencesla)

WRITER: Joe Beecroft (@thelocalperspective)

JACKSON'S BAR & BISTRO

OVERVIEW: This trendy bistro serves up food and drinks in the heart of Hillsboro Village.

COST: $$

ADDRESS: 1800 21st Ave S

NEIGHBORHOOD: Hillsboro Village

HOURS: Mon – Wed, 11am – 10pm
Thur, 11am – 11pm
Fri, 10am – 11pm
Sat – Sun, 9am – 11pm

PHONE: 1.615.385.9968

WEBSITE: jacksonsbarandbistro.com

INSTAGRAM: @jacksonsnash

ATMOSPHERE: It's dimly lit and artsy on the inside with a large covered patio. You'll find an eclectic, minimalist hipster vibe while retaining the neighborhood's comfortable, come-as-you-are environment.

HIGHLIGHTS: Personal favorites include the French toast (think stacked bread deep-fried and served funnel-cake style) and the Rio (grilled chicken, guacamole, and monterey jack).

INSIDER TIPS: 2-for-1 beers on weekdays from 3 to 6pm and half-price bottles of wine every Sunday afternoon and evening. There's even a dog-friendly patio!

PHOTOS (LEFT TO RIGHT):
Ashley W-F (@ashleylcm) and Jill & James (@eat.date.love)

WRITER: Kristen Shoates (@kristennicole86)

THE FLIPSIDE

OVERVIEW:
A modern, '50s-inspired diner in the heart of 12 South, The Flipside is known for their signature chicken dishes, milkshakes, craft beer, and plenty of those Nashville hip vibes.

COST: $$

ADDRESS: 2403 12th Ave S

NEIGHBORHOOD: 12 South

HOURS: Sat – Thur, 11am – 10pm
Fri, 11am – 2am

PHONE: 1.615.292.9299

WEBSITE: theflipside12south.com

INSTAGRAM: @theflipsidenash

COMMUNITY FAVORITE:
The menu is built around Jack's Best Chicken: thinly pounded and lightly breaded chicken breasts sautéed in olive oil and stacked with an array of creative toppings. Take, for example, The Memphis, covered with local barbecue sauce and bacon; The Elvis, topped with peanut butter and bananas; and The Popeye, a margarita-style dish with fresh mozzarella and balsamic.

PHOTOS (LEFT TO RIGHT):
Calia Minassian (@caliaflower)
Emerging Adult Eats (@emergingadulteats)
Juliana Wright (@ juliana_wright)
Trish Kozlak (@trishabelle_)

WRITER:
Kristen Shoates (@kristennicole86)

ATMOSPHERE:

Fun retro elements such as vintage Big Chill fridges, a soda counter, tall powder blue booths, and old Crosley/RCA signs give The Flipside an unforgettable flair, while its white exterior, modern high ceilings, and open garage doors keep it from being kitschy.

Casual and comfortable but situated in one of Nashville's trendiest neighborhoods, it's a popular spot among families and socialites alike.

HIGHLIGHTS:

You'll find the friendliest and most fun staff in Nashville! Everyone is consistently in a great mood and goes above and beyond to show you a great time too.

Three words: Tater Tot Nachos.

Bloody Mary fans, see the picture above and drool over all the goodies they embellish their bloodies with. It's safe to say you should put Flipside's Bloody Mary on your Nashville bucket list.

INSIDER TIPS:

Parking can be tough to find along the popular 12th South Avenue, but side streets offer ample street spots if you are prepared for a brief walk.

Friday night "Doo Wop to Hip Hop" dance parties feature a DJ playing hits from the '50s through today. Bring your dancing shoes. Check Instagram for upcoming dates as well as other events.

SUNFLOWER CAFE

OVERVIEW: This is the Nashville vegan community's answer to the all-prevalent meat-and-three. This cafeteria-style health stop will leave you feeling full—and craving more green in your diet. Local baked goods and fermented beverages (like kombucha) are often on the rotation.

COST: $$

ADDRESS: 2834 Azalea Pl

NEIGHBORHOOD: Berry Hill

HOURS: Mon – Thur, 11am – 9pm
Fri – Sat, 11am – 10pm

PHONE: 1.615.457.2568

WEBSITE: sunflowercafenashville.com

INSTAGRAM: @sunflowernash

ATMOSPHERE: It's a friendly, inviting space with covered and sunny outdoor seating.

HIGHLIGHTS: Try a veggie burger one of eight ways, with sesame kale on the side and curry chickpeas. The Thai ginger bowl with tofu over rice is also delicious. I usually ask for a taste of everything...

INSIDER TIPS: The staff is very friendly and will do combos of anything that looks tasty to you—even if it's not a traditional menu item. Don't forget about the outdoor seating on sunny days.

PHOTOS (LEFT TO RIGHT):
Alex Johnston (@alex_erin) and Andrea Rose (@andrea.m.rose)

WRITER: Alex Tapper (@fantasticmrtapp)

EPICE

OVERVIEW: With natural light, fresh Mediterranean food, and delicious wine, this place is a gem.

COST: $$

ADDRESS: 2902 12th Ave S

NEIGHBORHOOD: 12 South

HOURS: Tues – Sat, 11am – 10pm
Sun, 11am – 9pm

PHONE: 1.615.720.6765

WEBSITE: epicenashville.com

INSTAGRAM: @epicenashville

ATMOSPHERE: The space and the food are equally clean, crisp, and refreshing. You will feel like you are in a different country. The owner is fabulous and welcoming. You will be welcomed with warm smiles and natural light.

HIGHLIGHTS: Epice is open for brunch, lunch, and dinner. The food is so flavorful you won't even know it's good for you. There's a wonderfully curated wine and cocktail list.

INSIDER TIPS: Epice is easily one of the best restaurants in Nashville. The staff always has wonderful recommendations if you can't decide. The fish is the best I have had. The wine and cocktail selection is delightful. Reservations recommended, but even if you don't have one, try!

PHOTOS (LEFT TO RIGHT):
Karen Werthan (@Kwerthan) and Nate Erickson (@NATELY)

WRITER: Allison Holley (@appleandoaknash)

PINEWOOD SOCIAL

OVERVIEW:
Pinewood Social is a lively hangout perfect for all seasons and occasions. Locals gather for Sunday brunching, after-work happy hours, socials, family gatherings, and first dates. Pinewood Social serves up breakfast, lunch, and dinner. Activities range from bowling, bocce ball, coffee sipping, rounding up at the inside bar, or grabbing a spot in the courtyard by the pool.

COST: $$

ADDRESS: 33 Peabody St

NEIGHBORHOOD: Sobro

HOURS: Mon – Fri, 7am – 1am
Sat – Sun, 9am – 1am

PHONE: 1.615.751.8111

WEBSITE: pinewoodsocial.com

INSTAGRAM: @pinewoodsocial

COMMUNITY FAVORITE:
Without being too healthy, the Kale Caesar Salad, Fried Broccoli, and Jalapeño Mac and Cheese are definitely worth a try!

PHOTOS (LEFT TO RIGHT):
Gabrielle Cuoccio (@Gabreeyell)
Andrea Teggart (@luckyandi)
Sarah Polite (@NYCFoodieFinder)
Shannon Duggan (@shannondugganphotography)

WRITER:
Aubrey Hine (@aubreyhine)

ATMOSPHERE:

The vibe is a mix of rustic-hipster with just the right amount of modern familiar touches.

Your options are endless, with a coffee bar to greet you as you walk in, accompanied by a multitude of mix and matched tables and chairs. Venture to the bar and grab a one-of-a-kind cocktail from their spirits list before you head to the back to the vintage bowling alley. The outside courtyard ties the space together where friends and family gather to play games, lounge with a few beers by the pool, or start out their night early before heading downtown.

HIGHLIGHTS:

Pinewood Social caters to many events and is a great space to spend your entire day without the hustle and crowd of downtown Broadway. But if you have the Broadway itch, it's close enough to walk to after dinner and drinks.

INSIDER TIPS:

Bowling alley reservations don't come easy so make sure you plan ahead! The weekends are busy so be sure to snag a dinner reservation if you can.

There's plenty of parking available and it's FREE! But take an Uber or Lyft so you can try their tasty cocktails and stay awhile.

THE SMILING ELEPHANT

OVERVIEW: Visit The Smiling Elephant for a family-owned spot that features homemade Thai food.

COST: $

ADDRESS: 2213 8th Ave S

NEIGHBORHOOD: 8th Ave

HOURS: Mon - Thur, 11am - 2:30pm, 5 - 9pm
Fri, 11am -2:30pm, 4:30 - 9:30pm
Sat, 4:30 - 9:30pm

PHONE: 1.615.891.4488

WEBSITE: thesmilingelephant.com

INSTAGRAM: @smilingelephantnashville

ATMOSPHERE: Wood panels, bamboo, elephant trinkets, and celebrity-autographed photos adorn the walls. It's an semi-open kitchen, so be prepared to start salivating while you're waiting (patiently) in line.

HIGHLIGHTS: Start with the Tom Kha Soup. Definitely order a noodle dish—they're made from green beans! Pad Thai is a mainstay.

INSIDER TIPS: The Kopsombut family travels to Thailand a few times per year to do food research. So if you go when the family is traveling, just know that the limited menu is for the greater food.

PHOTOS (LEFT TO RIGHT):
Six Vegan Sisters (@sixvegansisters)
Abby Wharton (@tallblondeandhungry)

WRITER: Alex Tapper (@fantasticmrtapp)

THE WILD COW

OVERVIEW: The Wild Cow is a casual and affordable vegan and vegetarian restaurant with many gluten-free options.

COST: $

ADDRESS: 1896 Eastland Ave

NEIGHBORHOOD: East Nashville

HOURS: Wed – Mon, 11am – 10pm

PHONE: 1.615.262.2717

WEBSITE: thewildcow.com

INSTAGRAM: @thewildcow

ATMOSPHERE: A small intimate space with pictures of happy animals on the walls makes for a casual atmosphere.

HIGHLIGHTS: Most of their produce is grown locally and organic. They make almost all of their own sauces, dressings, soup stocks, etc. in-house. My personal favorite is their Taco Salad, it's HUGE and delicious... great for leftovers too. They donate 10% of their sales to charity each month.

INSIDER TIPS: Wednesday is Happy Hour— $1 off all beer and wine. Monday after 5pm is Burger and Beer Night—veggie burger, chips, and high gravity beer for $10.

PHOTOS (LEFT TO RIGHT):
Melissa McWilliams (@hangryvegan)
Tsouni Cooper (@yesitsallvegan)

WRITER: Abby Reuther (@abby.reuther)

TAVERN

OVERVIEW:
In the hustle and bustle of midtown, there lies Tavern—known for its hip brunch scene, drink specials, and not taking reservations. Tavern is Old Faithful—you're never disappointed, but it's always a guess as to how long you'll have to wait.

COST: $$

ADDRESS: 1904 Broadway

NEIGHBORHOOD: Midtown

HOURS: Mon - Thur, 11 - midnight
Fri, 11 - 3am
Sat, 10 - 3am
Sun, 10 - midnight

PHONE: 1.615.320.8580

WEBSITE: mstreetnashville.com/tavern/

INSTAGRAM: @tavernnashville

COMMUNITY FAVORITE:
For brunch, have Benedict Dos, but my bestie always raves about the Singapore Stir Fry (and wants to eat there every single weekend as if there are no other restaurants in Nashville).

PHOTOS (LEFT TO RIGHT):
Emily Mansfield (@emilyreadfields)
Meghan Edwards (@delish_duo)
Sara Draughon (@saradraughon)
Anthea Levi (@ThisIsItThough)

WRITER:
Sarah Patton (@sarahcharlottepatton)

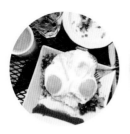

ATMOSPHERE:

Tavern has delicious food, but you can't go wrong with a patio to soak up some rays and lots of big screens to watch the games. It's packed with people of all ages. You can hear the crowd before you near the restaurant. Music is blaring and stories of last night's adventures are being discussed.

HIGHLIGHTS:

Honestly, there's never a bad time to dine at Tavern. Whether you're in the mood for lunch with the co-workers, celebrating a birthday dinner, or brunchin' with the girls—your palate won't be disappointed.

Try 2-for-1's on Thursdays from 2–10 on select wine, beer, and cocktails. 2-for-1's are also on Saturdays and Sundays during brunch (10am–3pm).

INSIDER TIPS:

Brunch at Tavern is amazing, but everyone else in Nashville thinks so too. Be prepared to wait at least an hour on the weekends, but that's totally fine because you can snag 2-for-1 cocktails at the bar. Oh, and if you don't have a big group, you can usually score seats at the bar, too. They have valet parking so don't even think about looking for parking in midtown. Or better yet, you should probably just Lyft or Uber if you're double fisting.

It's known as a favorite among celebrities—you never know who you'll be seated next to!

FIFTY FIRST KITCHEN & BAR

OVERVIEW: Here, you'll find dishes made from local and seasonal foods. Their menu ranges from small to large plates, with an emphasis on sharing.

COST: $$$

ADDRESS: 5104 Illinois Ave

NEIGHBORHOOD: The Nations

HOURS: Mon - Sat, bar opens at 4:30pm and dinner at 5:30pm

PHONE: 1.615.712.6111

WEBSITE: 51nashville.com

INSTAGRAM: @51nashville

ATMOSPHERE: It is a quaint restaurant located in a refurbished old house. The dimly lit interior and fireplace in the middle of the restaurant create a relaxing and intimate atmosphere. Outdoor seating is also available.

HIGHLIGHTS: I recommend starting with a charcuterie plate and their foccacia. Anything else off the menu is heavenly, ranging from salads and housemade pastas to fish and meat entrees.

INSIDER TIPS: Happy hour is 5:30-7pm Mon-Sat. Plates range from $4 to 9 with $5 beer selections and $7 specialty cocktails and wine. They have a dog park right next door! Grab a drink before you head to the dog park.

PHOTOS (LEFT TO RIGHT):
Anne Frazier (@anneelizabethfrazier)
Marie Antoinette Aviles (@bonjourantoinette)

WRITER: Holly Darnell (@hollywood_25)

OTAKU RAMEN

OVERVIEW: Otaku means obsession, which accurately describes the owner, Sarah's, relationship with noodles. Otaku South's roots began with her slinging bento boxes at the Farmer's Market and now she's the undisputed ramen queen of Nashville.

COST: $$

ADDRESS: 1104 Division St

NEIGHBORHOOD: The Gulch

HOURS: Tues – Thur, 11am – 3pm, 5 – 10pm
Fri, 11am – 3pm, 5pm – midnight
Sat, noon – midnight
Sun, noon – 10pm

PHONE: 1.615.94.8281

WEBSITE: otakuramen.com

INSTAGRAM: @otakusouthramen

ATMOSPHERE: Expect a sleek, minimal design with natural finishes and Japanese flair.

HIGHLIGHTS: Hands down, this is the best ramen in town. Add a spice bomb and/or soy egg. The Okonomiyaki sounds stranger than fiction, but tastes of umami dreams.

INSIDER TIPS: Otaku South is modeled after a traditional Japanese pup, or izakaya. Etiquette states that you order and eat quickly, especially if others are waiting. No reservations.

PHOTOS (LEFT TO RIGHT):
Christina Chintanaphol @christinamochi)
The Hangry Pharmacists (@hangrypharmacists)

WRITER: Alex Tapper (@fantasticmrtapp)

JOSEPHINE

OVERVIEW:
Josephine serves modern American cuisine in the most dreamy and stylish space.

COST: $$$

ADDRESS: 2316 12th Ave S

NEIGHBORHOOD: 12 South

HOURS: Mon – Thur, 5 – 10pm
Fri, 5 – 11pm
Sat, 10am – 11pm
Sun, 10am – 10pm

PHONE: 1.615.292.7766

WEBSITE: josephineon12th.com

INSTAGRAM: @josephineon12th

COMMUNITY FAVORITE:
Brunch: Bloody Mary and Josephine Benedict (poached eggs, scrapple, country ham, and brown butter hollandaise)

Dinner: Sweet Corn Ravioli (with mushrooms and herbs)

Dessert: Nutella Layer Cake (with candied hazelnut and orange peel)

PHOTOS (LEFT TO RIGHT):
Heather Hemmeger (@heatherhemmeger)
Paige Hardman (@paigehardman)
Sue-Jean Chun (@suej129)
Christine Mitchell (@gastrognomey)

WRITER: Abby Reuther (@abby.reuther)

ATMOSPHERE:

I value restaurants that are well designed. Don't get me wrong, the food is VERY important, but when a restaurant puts thought and detail into their design, it's another reason to come back, and come back often. Josephine has nailed both the food and atmosphere, so it's a win-win.

Their space is simple, with black and white floors, leather booths, long tables for community seating, and an open kitchen. It's beautiful and it gives me the interior design butterflies.

HIGHLIGHTS:

The food is beautiful. Is that even a thing? Well, yes, yes it is. The food always looks so pretty when it's placed in front of you, especially the dessert. So pretty, you might not want to eat it (just kidding—you'll devour it).

Brunchin' on the weekends is a big deal in Nashville and something we all take very seriously. Josephine does brunch, and does it well. Grab some friends, make a reservation, and eat and drink your hearts out—Saturday to Sunday from 10am to 3pm.

INSIDER TIPS:

Just like every restaurant in town, reservations are highly recommended. No one likes to wait to get their eat or drink on. So plan ahead and get on the schedule.

THE LITTLE DONKEY

OVERVIEW: This is a Mexican restaurant serving up fresh and made-from-scratch dishes.

COST: $$

ADDRESS: 1120 4th Ave N #103

NEIGHBORHOOD: Germantown

HOURS: Sun – Thur, 11am – 9:30pm
Fri – Sat, 11am – 10:30pm

PHONE: 1.615.567.5886

WEBSITE: thelittledonkey.com

INSTAGRAM: @littledonkeynash

ATMOSPHERE: The kitchen is completely exposed to the dining guests, leaving nothing unseen. When you go to order at the counter, you're guided by stacks of bagged corn to the register. These large bags are often dragged into the back so fresh tortillas can be made.

HIGHLIGHTS: A personal favorite of mine is the brisket taco, smoked in-house and balanced beautifully with onions, roasted poblano peppers, and queso fresco.

INSIDER TIPS: This may not be so well-known, but they have fantastic cocktails too. Their mojito is one of the best in town, and their signature Donkey's Daddy is a must-try.

PHOTOS (LEFT TO RIGHT):
Olivia Harrison (@Oliviaruth92)
Crystal De Luna-Bogan (@crystalrosebogan)

WRITER: Joe Beecroft (@thelocalperspective)

HEMINGWAY'S BAR & HIDEAWAY

OVERVIEW: A restaurant and bar inspired by Ernest Hemingway that serves refined tavern classics and craft cocktails.

COST: $$

ADDRESS: 438 Houston St, Suite 160

NEIGHBORHOOD: Wedgewood Houston

HOURS:
Lunch: Mon – Fri, 11am – 2:30pm
Dinner: Sun – Thurs, 5pm – 10pm
Fri – Sat, 5pm – 11pm
Brunch: Sat – Sun 10:30am – 2:30pm

Bar: Sun, 2:30pm – midnight
Mon – Thurs, 11am – midnight
Fri, 11am – 1am
Sat, 2:30pm – 1am

PHONE: 1.615.915.1715

WEBSITE: hemingwaysbarandhideaway.com

INSTAGRAM: @hemingwaysnash

ATMOSPHERE: Hemingway's is nestled in Houston Station, an old factory that a number of businesses now call home.

HIGHLIGHTS: They won a number of Nashville Scene awards in 2017, including #1 Best New Restaurant, #1 Best Bartender, #1 Best Mysterious Cocktail List, #2 Best New Bar, and #2 Best Cocktails.

INSIDER TIPS: It's perfect for a romantic date night or an intimate evening with friends.

PHOTOS: Abby Reuther (@abby.reuther)
WRITER: Abby Reuther (@abby.reuther)

MERCHANTS

OVERVIEW: Merchants is an iconic downtown restaurant with delicious food, thoughtful design, and fabulous atmosphere. Prime occasions include: dinner before the symphony; late-night creep after a Preds game; a downtown lunch between meetings.

COST: $$$

ADDRESS: 401 Broadway

NEIGHBORHOOD: Downtown

HOURS: Mon – Thur, 11am – 11pm
Fri, 11am – 1am
Sat, 10:30am – 1am
Sun, 10:30am – 11pm

PHONE: 1.615.254.1892

WEBSITE: merchantsrestaurant.com

ATMOSPHERE: Located in a historic building on Broadway, you'll find thoughtful nouveau Southern dinner fare and the best people-watching views in Nashville. On the first floor, sit at the copper-plated bar or in a booth. The second floor is a intimate formal dining room.

HIGHLIGHTS: Duck fat tater tots. I repeat: DUCK FAT TATER TOTS! Check out the Southern Fry, Grilled Salmon BLT, and the Chicken Fried Chicken too.

INSIDER TIPS: If you're looking for a more creative cocktail, give the bartenders a list of things you like and see what they come up with.

PHOTOS (LEFT TO RIGHT): Hope Bowling (@hope.bowling) and Josephine Parker (@ Missjosierose)

WRITER: Alex Tapper (@fantasticmrtapp)

THE SUTLER SALOON

OVERVIEW: This is a bar, restaurant, and live music venue that pays tribute to the past while offering unique Southern dishes, inventive cocktails, and chic lounge spaces for the new generation.

COST: $$

ADDRESS: 2600 Franklin Pike #109

NEIGHBORHOOD: Melrose

HOURS: Mon – Wed, 11am – midnight
Thur – Fri, 11am – 2am
Sat, 10am – 2am
Sun, 10am – 3pm

PHONE: 1.615.840.6124

WEBSITE: thesutler.com

INSTAGRAM: @thesutler

ATMOSPHERE: The main level has a saloon theme with a chic twist and features an open dining area along with a stage in the back. Downstairs is a speakeasy with velvet couches, creating a dark and cozy cocktail bar.

HIGHLIGHTS: The Sutler partnered with chef Nick Seabergh to design a menu that features modern takes on Southern staples.

INSIDER TIPS: Don't miss their Bluegrass Brunch, a popular event combining traditional Southern music with perhaps the most Southern institution of all: Sunday brunch.

PHOTOS (LEFT TO RIGHT): Lindsey Thom (@tindseylhom) and Abby Reuther (@abby.reuther)

WRITER: Kristen Shoates (@kristennicole86)

FIVE POINTS PIZZA

OVERVIEW:
Their homemade NY-style dough and tomato
sauce are made in-house, which is evident
as you take that delicious first pizza bite.
They offer pizza by the slice, whole pies,
and calzones, along with some yummy apps
and salads. Wine, beers on draft, and other
canned beers are available.

COST: $$

ADDRESS: 1012 Woodland St

NEIGHBORHOOD: East Nashville

HOURS:
Dine-In: Sun – Thur, 11am – 11pm
Fri – Sat, 11am – 12am
Late-Night Window:
Sun – Thur, 11pm – 1am
Fri – Sat, 12am – 3am

PHONE: 1.615.915.4174

WEBSITE: fivepointspizza.com

INSTAGRAM: @fivepointspizza

COMMUNITY FAVORITE:
The garlic knots are amazing—I always get a
1/2 order since I want to save some space for
the pizza. My go-to slice is the prosciutto and
basil.

PHOTOS (LEFT TO RIGHT):
Sammie Sok (@Soksammie)
Sarah Patton (@sarahcharlottepatton)
Zack Deaton (@Zackdeaton)
Shelby Buron (@shelbyburon)

WRITER:
Holly Darnell (@hollywood_25)

ATMOSPHERE:
Located in the heart of Five Points in East Nashville, the cozy restaurant has become a tried-and-true staple of the neighborhood. It is family-friendly and ushers you in with amazing smells of freshly baked dough. Tables comfortably seat anywhere from 2 to 6, with an outdoor patio in the back.

HIGHLIGHTS:
If you're with a group of people, I'd recommend ordering a whole pizza. I've had everything from the Old World to the Meatball Pie, and I have nothing but love for everything on the menu.

Lunch prices are legit (weekdays from 11am–2pm) and under $10. You can pick two slices and a drink, a slice and a salad, or the garlic knot and salad combination. Happy hour from 2–6pm doesn't disappoint either— you can get any slice paired with a draft beer for $8, or a cheese/pepperoni slice with a PBR for $5.

They also have a late-night walk-up window, where you can get a slice until 2am.

INSIDER TIPS:
Expect a little bit of a wait, especially on the weekends. If there is a wait, you can always put your name in, take a reservation buzzer and hit up one of the Five Points bars for a drink. If you're getting your slice or pie to go, there's a separate entrance on the right side of the restaurant. This way, you can avoid the restaurant crowd and get your to-go order more quickly.

HENRIETTA RED

OVERVIEW: An American restaurant offering contemporary cooking and an oyster bar.

COST: $$$

ADDRESS: 1200 4th Avenue North

NEIGHBORHOOD: Germantown

HOURS:
Dining Room: Tues – Sun, 5:30 – 10pm
Barroom: Tues – Thur, 5pm – midnight
Fri – Sat, 5pm – 1am
Sun, 5 – 10pm
Brunch: Sat – Sun, 10am – 2pm

PHONE: 1.615.490.8042

WEBSITE: henriettared.com

INSTAGRAM: @henrietta_red

ATMOSPHERE: Its mostly white and blue interior provides a coastal feel. It's divided into a dining room (complete with an oyster bar) and barroom.

HIGHLIGHTS: They focus on simple and fresh ingredients and many vegetable-forward dishes drive the menu. Oysters and shellfish are their expertise and you'll find a wide variety to choose from.

INSIDER TIPS: Whether you are in the dining room or barroom, I recommend getting a couple dishes and sharing. It's hard to choose a favorite off the menu. BUT make sure you don't leave without trying their oysters.

PHOTOS: Henrietta Red (@henrietta_red)

WRITER: Abby Reuther (@abby.reuther)

LOCKELAND TABLE

OVERVIEW: This charming East Nashville favorite features wood-fired pizzas and regionally sourced menu items.

COST: $$

ADDRESS: 1520 Woodland St

NEIGHBORHOOD: East Nashville

HOURS: Mon – Sat, 4 – 10pm

PHONE: 1.615.228.4864

WEBSITE: lockelandtable.com

INSTAGRAM: @lockelandtable

ATMOSPHERE: A cozy, community environment, this spot is a reflection of the Lockeland Springs neighborhood of East Nashville. Lockeland Table is truly lovely inside and out.

HIGHLIGHTS: The owner is also the head chef, so you know you're in good hands. Happy hour is Monday–Saturday from 4–6pm, which features a smaller menu of starters, cocktails, and options for children. A portion of the proceeds goes to the elementary school down the street.

INSIDER TIPS: The cheese pizza on the happy hour menu is a personal favorite pizza in Nashville! If you don't have a reservation (highly recommended), try during happy hour or grab a seat at the pizza bar.

PHOTOS (LEFT TO RIGHT):
Katelyn Burkhart Baker (@katelynburkhart)
Rachel Miklaszewski (@rachel.miklaszewski)

WRITER: Allison Holley (@appleandoaknash)

MARGOT CAFE & BAR

OVERVIEW: French and Italian cuisine with a menu that changes daily, featuring locally sourced ingredients.

COST: $$$

ADDRESS: 1017 Woodland St

NEIGHBORHOOD: East Nashville

HOURS: Tues – Sat, 5pm – 10pm
Sun, 11am – 2pm

PHONE: 1.615.227.4668

WEBSITE: margotcafe.com

INSTAGRAM: @margotcafe

ATMOSPHERE: It's housed in an old building that dates back to the 1930s. This cozy building is located in the Five Points area in the heart of East Nashville. Its exterior is surrounded by flower-filled gardens and the interior has brick walls decorated with copper pots and Italian vintage plates. It's the perfect place to have a quiet meal and glass of wine with a loved one.

HIGHLIGHTS: They have events—check out their calendar online. There's a great selection of French wines. Since their menu changes daily, you know that you'll get the freshest meal possible with quality ingredients.

INSIDER TIPS: Parking can be somewhat of a pain around the Five Points area, but if their lot is full you can usually find street parking on Woodland St and Clearview.

PHOTOS: Margot Cafe & Bar (@margotcafe)

WRITER: Abby Reuther (@abby.reuther)

FORT LOUISE

OVERVIEW: The coziest space, serving American classics with a fresh twist.

COST: $$

ADDRESS: 1304 McGavock Pike

NEIGHBORHOOD: East Nashville

HOURS: Tues – Thur, 4 – 10pm
Fri, 5 – 10pm
Sat – Sun, 10am – 3pm and 5 – 10pm

PHONE: 1.615.730.6273

WEBSITE: hungrylikeafort.com

INSTAGRAM: @hungrylikeafort

ATMOSPHERE: The moment I saw this adorable little bungalow converted into a restaurant, I knew it was special; then I walked inside and I knew I was in love. The interior is cozy, inviting, cheerful, and flooded with natural light. Outlining the whole interior is a cushioned bench covered with throw pillows; you will want to take a seat and not leave for hours.

HIGHLIGHTS: Brunch. It's a must. Their Challah French Toast is out of this world. It's a great place to go with a friend and share a handful of snacks . . . and don't forget the drinks. I recommend the Forgotten Summer.

INSIDER TIPS: If it's a warm day, take a seat outside on their back patio.

PHOTOS (LEFT TO RIGHT): Lesley Goldrich (@lesgoldrich) and Abby Reuther (@abby.reuther)

WRITER: Abby Reuther (@abby.reuther)

MARTIN'S BAR-B-QUE JOINT

OVERVIEW:
They focus on the legendary whole-hog BBQ tradition. Everything from their sides to their sauces are made from scratch every single day. You can guarantee your meal will be fresh and some of the best BBQ in Nashville.

COST: $$

ADDRESS: 410 4th Ave S
For other locations, please visit their website.

NEIGHBORHOOD: Downtown

HOURS: Every day, 11am – 10pm

PHONE: 1.615.288.0880

WEB SITE: martinsbbqjoint.com

INSTAGRAM: @martinsbbq

COMMUNITY FAVORITE:
The Pulled Pork Shoulder Tray comes with two sides—try my favorites, the mac 'n' cheese and green beans.

Another favorite is the Fried Chicken Tenders, which also comes with two sides.

Don't forget the Pecan Pie!

PHOTOS (LEFT TO RIGHT):
Adam Bohl (@adambohl)
Jessica Rothacker (@jessrothacker)
Alexa Coulton (@NashvilleRealtorista)
Abby Reuther (@abby.reuther)

WRITER:
Abby Reuther (@abby.reuther)

ATMOSPHERE:

There are four Nashville locations, but my personal favorite is their downtown location. A 13,000-square-foot space provides plenty of room to enjoy your BBQ or grab a drink. Order food on their first floor and grab a table. The second floor is a large beer garden with multiple bars and games like ping pong and shuffle board.

HIGHLIGHTS:

They've been featured on many popular TV networks and publications, so you know they're one of the best!

Everything is made from scratch daily, even the sides and sauces. But the bar-b-que process is actually started the day before, since the process for smoking a whole hog takes a long time and can't be rushed.

Martin's also has a great kids menu.

INSIDER TIPS:

You can buy their sauces and rubs online. I highly recommend the Sweet Dixie Bar-B-Que Sauce. It's their traditional, sweet, vinegar-tomato sauce that goes well with just about everything. They also have kitchen stuff, hats, and t-shirts.

Another website highlight is their recipe page, which provides recipes using their sauces and rubs. Find anything from BBQ Shrimp 'N' Grits to Alabama Pasta Salad.

Martin's is conveniently located near lower Broadway, so I highly recommend them for dinner and drinks before heading out for your big night on the town.

THE PHARMACY BURGER PARLOR & BEER GARDEN

OVERVIEW:
This burger, sausage, and soda joint is a Nashville must! Their unique burgers, homemade sausages, hand-crafted sodas, and locally sourced beer—that's a mouthful!—means The Pharmacy is one of Nashville's hottest locations.

COST: $$

ADDRESS: 731 Mcferrin Ave

NEIGHBORHOOD: East Nashville

HOURS: Sun - Thur, 11am - 10pm
Fri - Sat, 11am - 11pm

PHONE: 1.615.712.9517

WEBSITE: thepharmacynashville.com

INSTAGRAM: @thepharmacynashville

COMMUNITY FAVORITE:
The Stroganoff Burger, with caramelized onions, Swiss cheese, and mushroom stroganoff béchamel, is beyond good.

PHOTOS (LEFT TO RIGHT):
Alyssa Bantad (@Ayelyssadawn)
Abby Reuther (@abby.reuther)
Carly Cross (@carlycross)
Samuel A. Tallent (@Mrtallent21)

WRITER:
Joe Beecroft (@thelocalperspective)

ATMOSPHERE:

Being from England, I crave the pub and beer garden atmospheres. My delight when I found The Pharmacy was therefore beyond measure. Its exposed wooden beams are a close cry to some of England's oldest establishments. The beer garden, I dare say, beats most English beer gardens. Its beautiful greenery, landscaping, ample seating, and low-hanging light bulbs makes this somewhere I can sit for hours.

HIGHLIGHTS:

Their local beer selection changes all the time, but their staff are always very knowledgeable about what's being served. All sodas are made in-house from scratch and I would certainly suggest trying one—call it dessert. My perfect Pharmacy trip is a pint and burger in the beer garden just as the sun begins to go down—as English as it comes!

INSIDER TIPS:

Rule 1: The Pharmacy is ALWAYS busy. When you read this and think to yourself, "Ah, we will just go on a Tuesday/Wednesday night," then please re-read Rule 1. With that being said, it should not deter you from going. They are great at getting you seated in a timely fashion. You could always throw your name down and then grab a drink at the bar. I must reiterate though, that when you come to Nashville, The Pharmacy should be at the top of your list.

URBAN GRUB

OVERVIEW: Urban Grub serves Southern traditional plates with a twist of their own, and is known for their amazing fresh seafood, oysters, and meats.

COST: $$$

ADDRESS: 2506 12th Ave S

NEIGHBORHOOD: 12 South

HOURS: Tues – Thur, 4pm – 1am
Fri, 4pm – 2am
Sat, 11 – 2am
Sun, 11 – midnight

PHONE: 1.615.679.9342

WEBSITE: urbangrub.net

INSTAGRAM: @urban_grub

ATMOSPHERE: The exterior architecture catches your eye as you drive through the busy 12 South area. Dim lighting and dark/warm decor make it the perfect place for a date night or intimate conversation. There's also a great outdoor seating area with greenery and strings of lights above.

HIGHLIGHTS: The wine and craft cocktail list is impressive. Their oysters are delicious, and that says a lot because I'm not too fond of oysters. They also have a great oyster bar that's perfect for being right in the action.

INSIDER TIPS: Make a reservation—especially during brunch on the weekends.

PHOTOS (LEFT TO RIGHT):
Amy Gardner (@a_ngardner) and Alexandra G. Jalil (@alexandrajalil)

WRITER: Abby Reuther (@abby.reuther)

ROLF & DAUGHTERS

OVERVIEW: This spot is known for their extraordinary chef, thoughtful dishes, seasonal ingredients, and housemade pasta.

COST: $$$

ADDRESS: 700 Taylor St

NEIGHBORHOOD: Germantown

HOURS: Every day, 5:30 – 10pm

PHONE: 1.615.866.9897

WEBSITE: rolfanddaughters.com

INSTAGRAM: @rolfanddaughters

ATMOSPHERE: The location, a renovated factory boiler room, makes for a cozy/industrial vibe. There's indoor and outdoor seating.

HIGHLIGHTS: The ingredients are fresh, local, and seasonal. Sharing is encouraged. Try the excellent cocktails and wine pairings.

INSIDER TIPS: It's highly recommended that you make a reservation, but if you are a party of two and you get there early, you can usually find a seat at the bar; otherwise it's worth the wait. You probably won't know what most of the ingredients are but the staff is super helpful and they never make you feel like a food dummy. The menu changes seasonally, but if they have the Mushroom Alfredo, get it. The Beef Tartare is on-point, but then again, so is everything else.

PHOTOS (LEFT TO RIGHT):
Darren Jackson (@darren2112) and Holly Y. (@hamburgerholly)

WRITER: Allison Holley (@appleandoaknash)

HATTIE B'S HOT CHICKEN

OVERVIEW:
If you haven't been to Hattie B's, then you're missing out. Hot chicken is a Nashville staple and Hattie B's does it all right.

COST: $

ADDRESS: 5209 Charlotte Pike
For their other location, please visit the website.

NEIGHBORHOOD: Sylvan Park

HOURS: Mon – Thur, 11am – 10pm
Fri – Sat, 11am – midnight
Sun, 11am – 4pm

PHONE: 1.615.712.7137

WEBSITE: hattieb.com

INSTAGRAM: @hattiebs

COMMUNITY FAVORITE:
For brunch, try the Jumbo Tenders & Waffles. Mild Tenders are the lunch pick. Pimento Mac & Cheese and the Baked Beans are excellent, and you can't miss the Banana Pudding.

PHOTOS (LEFT TO RIGHT):
Emily Cutrer and Lee Gabardi (@EmileelandTravels)
Nicole Brodie (@nicolechristel)
Mary Beth Wallace (@mbwallace93)
Joanna Lukaszewska (@Joannalukaszewska)

WRITER:
Abby Reuther (@abby.reuther)

ATMOSPHERE:
Just what you'd expect out of a Southern hot chicken restaurant—casual, laid-back, and family friendly. Order at the counter and grab a seat at the large picnic tables. There's outdoor seating available for those of you who need a breeze as you scarf down that hot chicken.

HIGHLIGHTS:
The chicken comes in five different "hot" levels, guaranteeing the perfect level for everyone. The five levels are: the Southern (no heat), mild/medium, hot, damn hot, and Shut The Cluck Up (for all those brave souls out there). I'm not a huge fan of spice (I know, I know...) so I'm a fan of the mild/medium, which gives me the perfect amount of spice.

The brunch is my personal favorite. I love the sweet and spicy combination that chicken and waffles provides. Brunch is available ONLY on Sundays and there is usually a long line waiting outside before the doors open, so get there early.

INSIDER TIPS:
Get there early, especially on the weekends, and expect to wait in line. It's worth the wait—believe me. Take advantage of the wait and get to know your neighbor in line. Everyone is usually friendly and you never know who you'll meet. Look at the menu beforehand. Don't be that person who gets to the counter and needs 5 minutes to review the menu before ordering.

CAFE ROZE

OVERVIEW: A dreamy all-day cafe serving American classics plus speciality coffees and drinks.

COST: $

ADDRESS: 1115 Porter Rd

NEIGHBORHOOD: East Nashville

HOURS: Mon – Sat, 8am – midnight
Sun, 8am – 10pm

PHONE: 1.615.645.9100

WEBSITE: caferoze.com

INSTAGRAM: @caferoze

ATMOSPHERE: The cafe is full of rose tones, concrete walls, fresh flowers, high ceilings, and lots of natural light. This dreamy spot is an inviting place for catching up with friends, grabbing a coffee solo, or having the perfect date night.

HIGHLIGHTS: For breakfast/brunch, you must try the Matcha Latte and Savory Oats. For lunch, a Roze Bowl and Pinewood Farms Grass-Fed Burger. For dinner, the Vesper cocktail, Avocado Hummus, and Farro Risotto.

INSIDER TIPS: This place is every blogger's and Instagramer's dream location to take photos. You really can't take a bad Instagram photo in this place. Post away and be sure to tag @TheNashvilleGuide.

PHOTOS (LEFT TO RIGHT): Abby Reuther (@abby.reuther) and Lesley Goldrich (@lesgoldrich)

WRITER: Abby Reuther (@abby.reuther)

ARNOLD'S COUNTRY KITCHEN

OVERVIEW: The reigning meat-and-three king—this is old Nashville, and it's better eats than any farm-to-table trend or food truck craze.

COST: $

ADDRESS: 605 8th Ave S
For their other location, please visit the website.

NEIGHBORHOOD: The Gulch

HOURS: Mon – Fri, 10:30 – 2:45pm

PHONE: 1.615.256.4455

WEBSITE: arnoldscountrykitchen.com

INSTAGRAM: @arnoldscountrykitchen

ATMOSPHERE: The line out the door every day at lunch and the walls adorned with family photos and media accolades tell you half the story, and the Banana Pudding does the rest. It's simple. Get in line, pick your food, grab the sweet tea, and find a spot. Somehow there's always one spot with your name on it.

HIGHLIGHTS: The Mac 'n' Cheese is considered currency.

INSIDER TIPS: Try to get there right at 10:30am for an early lunch and a larger table. Do not skip dessert (hint: Banana Pudding).

PHOTOS (LEFT TO RIGHT):
Meredith Sloan (@mrssloan1988)
Jessica Hill (@Jhill1)

WRITER: Kelley Griggs (@kelleyboothe)

5TH & TAYLOR

OVERVIEW:
This American restaurant does a marvelous job of effortless dining, set in an outstanding space. It's a class act.

COST: $$$

ADDRESS: 1411 5th Ave N

NEIGHBORHOOD: Germantown

HOURS: Mon - Thur, 5 - 10pm
Fri - Sat, 5pm - midnight
Sun, 10:30am - 2pm, 5 - 9pm

PHONE: 1.615.242.4747

WEBSITE: 5thandtaylor.com

INSTAGRAM: @5thandtaylor

COMMUNITY FAVORITE:
Try the Bacon Wrapped Quail—it's salty and sweet, juicy and crispy—all areas of the palate are hit with this appetizer.

Don't miss the Beef Cheek Pot Roast. The meat falls apart and melts in your mouth. The gravy is so rich and the potatoes are always mashed to perfection (you know—smooth).

PHOTOS (LEFT TO RIGHT):
Radhika & Indera Joshi (@ittakestwo2mango)
Caroline Kiesling (@tastyytn)
Julia Severino (@julescapade)
Nicole Rossi (@nicolerossi)

WRITER:
Joe Beecroft (@thelocalperspective)

ATMOSPHERE:

Situated inside an incredible, industrial space in Germantown, its high, wooden ceilings, exposed brick, and visible metal framing creates a wonderful setting for dinner or brunch.

They also have a wonderful patio. Sheltered away from the hustle and bustle of a normal day by a gorgeous planted tree line, the patio also features a magnificent fountain—let the noise of water and the privacy of the patio sooth your soul.

HIGHLIGHTS:

Service is always immaculate at 5th & Taylor, with the staff being extremely knowledgeable of the food and drinks they offer.

All the food and drinks are amazing and you won't be disappointed with anything you order. Don't skip out on dessert! They have a large dessert and dessert cocktail menu.

INSIDER TIPS:

I'd recommend a reservation, but for the class this restaurant oozes, its an incredibly fulfilling experience worth the time. They do a fantastic valet service that eliminates the need to park.

On nice days, definitely take advantage of their large patio.

SALT & VINE

OVERVIEW: A gourmet marketplace, restaurant, and wine bar makes Salt & Vine a Nashville one-of-a-kind.

COST: $$

ADDRESS: 4001 Charlotte Ave

NEIGHBORHOOD: Sylvan Park

HOURS: Mon – Thur, 8am – 10pm
Fri – Sat, 8am – 11pm

PHONE: 1.615.800.8517

WEBSITE: saltandvinenashville.com

INSTAGRAM: @saltandvinenashville

ATMOSPHERE: Enjoy a clean, crisp interior with pops of bright yellow and greenery. You'll find yourself sipping fine wine, eating specialty cheeses, and not wanting to leave.

HIGHLIGHTS: The list includes gourmet prepared foods, a seasonal small plate dining menu, tasting room, cured meats and cheeses, spiced lamb meatballs, artisan chocolate board, 25 wines offered by the glass or bottle—and the list could go on and on.

INSIDER TIPS: If you're not knowledgeable with wine or wine pairings, don't let that stop you from experiencing new kinds and flavors. The staff is super knowledgeable about wine and what pairs well with each kind.

PHOTOS (LEFT TO RIGHT):
Abby Hester (@abbyotthester)
Oksana Chernitskiy (@OksanaChernitskiy)

WRITER: Abby Reuther (@abby.reuther)

NIGHT TRAIN PIZZA

OVERVIEW: Night Train is an oven-fired pizza and beer joint.

COST: $

ADDRESS: 600 9th Ave S, Suite 100

NEIGHBORHOOD: The Gulch

HOURS: Sun – Thurs, 11am – 9pm
Fri – Sat, 11am – 10pm

PHONE: 1.615.540.0138

WEBSITE: nighttrainpizza.com

INSTAGRAM: @nighttrainpizza

ATMOSPHERE: The vibe is a classic pizza restaurant with red and white plaid tablecloths, pizza sign, and a wall of beer cans: super laid back.

HIGHLIGHTS: They have an amazing brunch on the weekends between 11am and 2pm, complete with cheap and delicious Bloody Marys and Mimosas!

INSIDER TIPS: Monday through Friday from 11am to 3pm, cheese and pepperoni slices are super cheap.

PHOTOS: Abby Reuther (@abby.reuther)

WRITER: Abby Reuther (@abby.reuther)

BURGER UP

OVERVIEW:
This is the friendliest burger joint in town that knows, loves, and values their farmers, staff, and customers. Specializing in inventive burgers made from locally sourced meats and ingredients, Burger Up is also the home of some of the best fries in town.

COST: $$

ADDRESS: 2901 12th Ave S
For their other location, please visit the website.

NEIGHBORHOOD: 12 South

HOURS: Every day, 11am – 10pm

PHONE: 1.615.279.3767

WEBSITE: burger-up.com

INSTAGRAM: @burgerup

COMMUNITY FAVORITE:
Try the Bison Burger. Vegetarian will enjoy the Marathon Burger. Don't miss the Truffle Fries or Kale Salad.

PHOTOS (LEFT TO RIGHT):
Aleq Bateman (@aleqbateman)
Caroline Kiesling (@tastyytn)
Abbygayle Baker, Emma Beck, Mason Zgoda (@eatgros)
Kathryn Tilmes (@kathryntilmes)

WRITER:
Kate Moore (@moore_kate)

ATMOSPHERE:

Walking in the doors of Burger Up is like walking into a group of friends that is super welcoming. The staff is laid back, way cooler than me, and super kind.

HIGHLIGHTS:

They use local farmers and resources (including my friends at Porter Road Butcher and The Peach Truck), which makes me feel proud to buy an additional cocktail and side salad.

I don't make a trip to Burger Up without ordering the Truffle Fries. And I make SURE to top them with their homemade aioli and ketchup. Let's talk Kale Salad too. It's perfect—salty from the pecorino romano, sweet from the dried cherries, tangy from the citrus vinaigrette, crunchy from the roasted hazelnuts. And then you top it with a Bison Burger patty or salmon. Oh, and a side of Truffle Fries. Always a side of Truffle Fries. Their cocktails are on-point too—get the special.

INSIDER TIPS:

Sit at the bar. Become part of the Burger Up family. Begin your meal with an order of Sweet Potato Fries. Order anything at all on the menu.

My Mom's insider tip is to order the Onion Rings and a rare burger patty. She's from the South, y'all, and she knows her onion rings and ground beef.

ADELE'S

OVERVIEW:
This is celebrity chef Jonathan Waxman's first restaurant in Nashville. Adele's is named after his mother and has a menu inspired by his mother's cooking. It's fine American food with a Southern kick, and it's a Nashville bucket list must.

COST: $$

ADDRESS: 1210 McGavock St

NEIGHBORHOOD: The Gulch

HOURS: Mon - Thur, 5 - 10pm
Fri, 11:30am - 3pm, 5 - 11pm
Sat, 11am - 3pm, 5 - 11pm
Sun, 10:30am - 2:30pm, 5 - 9pm

PHONE: 1.615.988.9700

WEBSITE: adelesnashville.com

INSTAGRAM: @adelesnashville

COMMUNITY FAVORITE:
Try the Spike cocktail: Spike, Heroes vodka, organic watermelon, and mint. For dinner, order the Gnocchi—including delicate squash, corn, rosemary, and grana.

PHOTOS (LEFT TO RIGHT):
Ashley Couse (@bloomandnourish)
Mikey Lee (@Tsubi.lee)
Aubrey Hine (@aubreyhine)
Andra Turner (@andratee)

WRITER:
Abby Reuther (@abby.reuther)

ATMOSPHERE:

It's a large open concept, with high ceilings and many garage doors to provide the most magical natural light. On nice days, the doors are open and the breeze flows through, making the inside feel like one giant patio. Speaking of patios, they also have a patio perfect for taking in the Nashville city skylines.

My personal favorite decor touch is their bright teal bar stools, which add that perfect pop of color and charm. You'll never guess that the building used to house an auto repair shop!

HIGHLIGHTS:

Waxman focuses on seasonal dishes with the ingredients sourced from local farms— guaranteeing you the very best quality.

The Sunday Brunch Buffet is a must, trust me.

Enjoy local brews from Little Harpeth Brewing, Jackalope Brewing Company, and more.

INSIDER TIPS:

With the quality, atmosphere, and service, it's no surprise that Adele's is a celebrity favorite. I've heard Reese Witherspoon is known to pop up in the restaurant every now and then.

Parking is limited and is a hassle in The Gulch, so take advantage of the valet service.

Reservations are highly recommended, but if you go last-minute, try and grab a bar seat— it's a first-come first-served spot.

Did I mention you should go for the Sunday Brunch Buffet?

BUTCHER & BEE

OVERVIEW: Butcher & Bee features eclectic foods with exquisite presentation and Mediterranean flair. Plates are a little on the small side, which gives you the perfect opportunity to sample and share.

COST: $$

ADDRESS: 902 Main St

NEIGHBORHOOD: East Nashville

HOURS: Lunch: Mon – Sat, 11am – 2pm
Dinner: Sun – Thur, 5 – 11pm
Fri – Sat, 5pm – midnight
Brunch: Sun, 10am – 2pm

PHONE: 1.615.226.3322

WEBSITE: butcherandbee.com

INSTAGRAM: @bandbnashville

ATMOSPHERE: With colorful decor and knowledgeable staff, it's typically filled with a mix of locals and visitors—foodies of all types who come for the unique fare.

HIGHLIGHTS: Don't miss the Whipped Feta as a starter—or the Mmm...This Is A Tasty Burger! Tiger-Style Brussels are a must. Seared Wild Mushrooms are a hearty veggie option.

INSIDER TIPS: Order to share. The small plates are cheaper if you order more of them. The covered patio is great on a nice day. Don't overlook the cocktail menu.

PHOTOS (LEFT TO RIGHT):
Caitlin Morgan (@caitiepotatey) and Nicole Gerstenkorn (@nickage_)

WRITER: Alex Tapper (@fantasticmrtapp)

MONELL'S DINING & CATERING

OVERVIEW: Monell's is all-you-can-eat Southern comfort food served family-style at communal tables in a Victorian house.

COST: $

ADDRESS: 1235 6th Ave N
For their other location, please visit the website.

NEIGHBORHOOD: Germantown

HOURS: Mon, 7am – 3pm
Tues – Fri, 7am – 8:30pm
Sat, 8am – 8:30pm
Sun, noon – 3am and 8am – 4pm

PHONE: 1.615.248.4747

WEBSITE: monellstn.com

INSTAGRAM: @monellstn

ATMOSPHERE: The staff asks for no cellphones at the table for good reason. The table is a chance to talk to a neighbor, a stranger, a tourist, to learn something interesting and try something new. Relax and get to know the world.

HIGHLIGHTS: Don't miss the brunch, with fried chicken, coffee, pancakes piled high with maple syrup, potatoes, sausages, bacon, biscuits and gravy.

INSIDER TIPS: Take advantage of the communal tables—get to know your neighbors.

PHOTOS (LEFT TO RIGHT):
Nicole Chiu (@chiumonster) and Abby Reuther (@abby.reuther)

WRITER: Kelley Griggs (@kelleyboothe)

CITY HOUSE

OVERVIEW:
This is arguably Nashville's BEST restaurant, our city's James Beard–award-winning establishment, featuring Italian food with a Southern flair. I could write for days here but words will not do this restaurant justice—your visit will, however.

COST: $$

ADDRESS: 1222 4th Ave N

NEIGHBORHOOD: Germantown

HOURS:
Mon, 5 - 10pm
Wed - Sat, 5 - 10pm
Sun, 5 - 9pm

PHONE: 1.615.736.5838

WEBSITE: cityhousenashville.com

INSTAGRAM: @cityhousenashville

COMMUNITY FAVORITE:
Belly Ham Pizza is the best pizza in America (belly ham, mozzarella, grana padano, oregano, and chilies, topped with a sunny side egg in the middle).

PHOTOS (LEFT TO RIGHT):
Sarah Yi (@cle_eats)
Allisyn K. Morgan (@allisynkmorgan)
Derrick Rice (@rice_dl)
Jennifer Kite | SCOUT-small discoveries (@scoutbaby)

WRITER:
Joe Beecroft (@thelocalperspective)

ATMOSPHERE:

Think a European farmhouse meets America's industrial past. Its white-washed brick and tall windows could put City House in the Swiss Alps. The interior decor is also industrial farmhouse, creating a dining room that is truly beautiful. The kitchen is visible to all who visit and from it arises the sound of bustle and wafts of Italian aromas, filling the heads in the room with day dreams of pizza and salivating mouths.

HIGHLIGHTS:

I must state that any dish you get from City House is going to be amazing. I've yet to try something that I haven't loved.

Their menu is seasonal, so it's a nice treat to see something new on the menu each time you go. Plus you know it's going to be made fresh with the best local, in-season ingredients.

Always listen to the deserts on offer too— they're simply divine.

INSIDER TIPS:

Nashville has the perfect mix of street food and fine dining and if you want to do a fine dining experience, make sure it's City House. It's very reasonable and I recommend ordering multiple dishes and sharing. The more dishes you can taste, the better. A reservation is recommended for busier days but you can walk in if you're willing to sit at the bar. They let you bring in your own wine for a corkage fee.

AVO

OVERVIEW:
This healthy raw vegan restaurant provides meals from locally sourced ingredients.

COST: $$

ADDRESS: 3 City Ave Suite #200

NEIGHBORHOOD: Midtown

HOURS: Mon – Sat, 11am – 9pm

PHONE: 1.615.329.2377

WEBSITE: eatavo.com

INSTAGRAM: @eatavo

COMMUNITY FAVORITE:
For brunch, try the Avo Toast (sprouted, raw pecan flat bread topped with avocado spread, chimichurri sauce, tomato, hemp, fresh herbs, and marinated cold-smoked coconut). For dinner, order the Lasagna (marinated zucchini, cashew hemp seed ricotta, basil pesto, and sun-dried tomato sauce). If you'd like a drink, try the AVOcado Margarita (AVO's signature cocktail made with fresh avocado, resposado, cilantro, fresh lime, agave, and housemade orange dust).

PHOTOS (LEFT TO RIGHT):
Katje Lael (@theoilmuse)
Holly Darnell (@hollywood_25)
Amanda Trott Usery (@trottinginheels)
Sarah Patton (@sarahcharlottepatton)

WRITER:
Abby Reuther (@abby.reuther)

ATMOSPHERE:

From the exterior, you'll notice this restaurant appears to be housed in a large shipping container—strange but awesome at the same time! The outside is painted with a mural of avocados, which has become a famous photo op for visitors.

The interior is small but clean, crisp, and filled with natural light. The bar backdrop is a "living" wall filled with plants. Also, inside is a small marketplace where you can buy healthy eats and products.

There's a small outside patio out back with lights streaming above and outlined with flowers. It's cozy and magical.

HIGHLIGHTS:

They strive to source the absolute finest plant-based ingredients from local farms and sustainable businesses in order to feed the Nashville community with the most health-promoting foods possible. With that, the menu items change based on what's currently in season. The menu is ENTIRELY plant-based and they don't use any processed ingredients.

INSIDER TIPS:

Get the AVOcado Margarita—even if you don't like avocados. It's a creamy dream and you'll be ready to order a second.

Their portions are perfect. I always leave feeling completely satisfied without that stuffed feeling.

EDLEY'S BAR-B-QUE

OVERVIEW: "A tribute to all things Southern"; they smoke their BBQ daily. It's the freshest-tasting smoked meat in Nashville.

COST: $

ADDRESS: 908 Main St
For other locations, please visit their website.

NEIGHBORHOOD: East Nashville

HOURS: Every day, 11am - 10pm

PHONE: 1.615.873.4085

WEBSITE: edleysbbq.com

INSTAGRAM: @edleysbbq

ATMOSPHERE: You're instantly greeted with a sweet smoky scent. The build and decor pays homage to what imbues their meat with smoke–the wood. They also have a great outdoor covered seating area.

HIGHLIGHTS: They prepare many Southern-style side dishes to accompany your choice of meat. They also have a great selection of local beers. And their homemade BBQ sauce–don't even get me started!

INSIDER TIPS: Get the Smoked Brisket Sandwich with Mac 'n' Cheese and Jalapeño Corn Bread. I order this literally every time I go.

PHOTOS (LEFT TO RIGHT):
Caroline LeGates (@goodeatswithcaro)
and Matthew Griffith (@m_h_griffith)

WRITER: Joe Beecroft (@thelocalperspective)

food trucks

THE GRILLED CHEESERIE

OVERVIEW: A local-trotting pair of food trucks serving an array of heavenly grilled cheese combinations, crispy side items, and homemade desserts.

COST: $

ADDRESS: Mobile truck. *Please visit their website for the weekly schedule.*

WEBSITE: grilledcheeserie.com

INSTAGRAM: @thegrilledcheeserie

HIGHLIGHTS: The Pimento Mac & Chee is an absolute necessity. And whatever you do, always get the tots with homemade ketchup. You can make your own grilled cheese if you please—with a multitude of bread, cheese, and 5-star added toppings like smoked jalapeño relish, heritage bacon, and caramelized onions.

Their brick-and-mortar, The Grilled Cheeserie Melt Shop, is in Hillsboro Village (2003 Belcourt Ave).

INSIDER TIPS: If you don't feel like chasing down the truck, The Grilled Cheeserie is also available on OrderUp or a weekly delivery option. They also have a new brick-and-mortar location in Hillsboro Village.

PHOTOS (LEFT TO RIGHT):
Darren Jackson (@darren2112)
Kathleen Clipper (@thenewgirlinnashville)

WRITER: Aubrey Hine (@aubreyhine)

BRADLEY'S CURBSIDE CREAMERY

OVERVIEW: Serving up ice cream, shakes, and floats in the streets of Nashville. They say it perfectly themselves: "Ice cream doesn't have to be fancy. It just needs to be good. And that's what you'll get with every scoop—simple, timeless, delicious ice cream."

COST: $

ADDRESS: Mobile truck. *Please visit their website for the weekly schedule.*

WEBSITE: bradleyscreamery.com

INSTAGRAM: @bradleyscreamery

HIGHLIGHTS: They strive to serve ice cream flavored with real fruit and quality ingredients, inspired by old-fashioned Southern favorites that will quickly become some of your new favorites as well.

INSIDER TIPS: Sometimes they have specialty flavors, while they last, so be sure to keep an eye out for those. Some examples are Pumpkin Spice, Cotton Candy, and Mango Sorbet—YUM, just YUM.

PHOTOS (LEFT TO RIGHT):
Makayla Knight (@foxhipfashion)
Grace Willis (@itsgracewillis)

WRITER: Abby Reuther (@abby.reuther)

BARE NAKED BAGEL

OVERVIEW: Bare Naked Bagel brings New York straight to the streets of Nashville by serving New York–style bagels and bagel sandwiches made from locally sourced ingredients.

COST: $

ADDRESS: Mobile truck. *Please visit their website for the weekly schedule.*

WEBSITE: barenakedbagel.com

INSTAGRAM: @barenakedbagel

HIGHLIGHTS: Just because it's bagels, don't think they only serve breakfast items—they also serve unique lunch and dinner options.

They are committed to using fresh, local, unprocessed ingredients, and this makes me love them even more.

INSIDER TIPS: If you need some inspiration on what to order, my go-to is The Breakfast, a bagel sandwich with either a fried or scrambled egg with cheddar cheese, and add bacon (always add bacon). Or if I'm feeling a little edgy, I'll order the Avocado Boast, an open-face bagel with avocado spread, jalapeño, pickled red onions, roasted red peppers, toasted pumpkin seeds, and feta cheese.

PHOTOS(LEFT TO RIGHT):
Aubrey Hine (@aubreyhine)
Holly Darnell (@hollywood_25)

WRITER: Abby Reuther (@abby.reuther)

FUNK SEOUL BROTHER

OVERVIEW: It's a Korean-inspired restaurant rolling on four wheels. They serve up sushi burritos, Korean fried chicken, Korean BBQ tacos, and much more mouth-watering eats.

COST: $$

ADDRESS: Mobile truck. *Please visit their website for the weekly schedule.*

WEBSITE: funkseoultruck.com

INSTAGRAM: @funkseoultruck

HIGHLIGHTS: Pretty much everything on their menu is a highlight item, but you have to try one of their sushi burritos. My go-to is the Spicy Tuna Sushi Burrito.

Whatever you do, don't forget the Angry Tots, which are tater tots with gochujang BBQ sauce, sriracha aioli, and ginger scallion salsa.

INSIDER TIPS: Visit their website to view their food truck schedule.

PHOTOS (LEFT TO RIGHT):
Lauren Portice (@hangry_sisters)
Sawyer Wilson (@sawyerismyfirstname)

WRITER: Abby Reuther (@abby.reuther)

EAT + DRINK

dessert

BOBBIE'S DAIRY DIP

OVERVIEW: Bobbie's is a Nashville classic since 1951 that still has that '50s charm. They're known for their tasty ice cream cones, burgers, and fries.

COST: $

ADDRESS: 5301 Charlotte Ave
For their other location, please visit the website.

NEIGHBORHOOD: Sylvan Park

HOURS: Mon – Thur, 11am – 7pm
Fri – Sat, 11am – 8pm

PHONE: 1.615.463.8088

WEBSITE:
facebook.com/bobbiesdairydipcharlotteave

INSTAGRAM: @bobbiesdairy

ATMOSPHERE: There's a walk-up order window with outdoor picnic table seating—definitely laid back and perfect for those casual days.

HIGHLIGHTS: It's only open during summer, so it's always a special treat when it opens back up. My favorite meal is their Black Bean Burger, topped with guacamole, jalapeños, and salsa, and a vanilla ice cream cone with sprinkles.

INSIDER TIPS: The line can be long but don't let that discourage you because the service is fast. There's also a downtown location.

PHOTOS (LEFT TO RIGHT):
Allison Elefante (@rubyandpeach)
and Mali Schneiter (@malikathleen)

WRITER: Abby Reuther (@abby.reuther)

THE CUPCAKE COLLECTION

OVERVIEW: This family-owned cupcake shop sells a variety of flavors, including specialty flavors of the week.

COST: $

ADDRESS: 1213 6th Ave N
For their other location, please visit the website.

NEIGHBORHOOD: Germantown

HOURS: Mon, 9:30 – 4:30pm
Tues – Thur, 9:30 – 5:30pm
Fri, 9:30am – 4:30pm
Sun, 11am – 4pm

PHONE: 1.615.244.2900

WEBSITE: thecupcakecollection.com

INSTAGRAM: @thecupcakecollection

ATMOSPHERE: The Cupcake Collection is a small, quaint, old house nestled into the Germantown neighborhood. Upon walking in the door, smiling faces and the smell of freshly baked cupcakes greet you.

HIGHLIGHTS: Their cupcakes have the perfect ratio of cake to frosting. Gluten-free and vegan cupcakes are also available.

INSIDER TIPS: They also provide catering for weddings, birthday parties, etc.

PHOTOS (LEFT TO RIGHT):
Marc Cowans (@Marcc856)
Taylor Hartman (@taylorhart15)

WRITER: Holly Darnell (@hollywood_25)

JAKE'S BAKES

OVERVIEW: Get warm cookies delivered right to your doorstep or visit them at their store to check out all their cookie flavors in the cookie case.

COST: $

ADDRESS: 2422 Elliston Pl

NEIGHBORHOOD: Elliston Place

HOURS: *For seasonal hours, please visit their website.*

PHONE: 1.615.645.5916

WEBSITE: jakesbakesnashville.com

INSTAGRAM: @jakesbakes

ATMOSPHERE: Enjoy warm baked cookies right from the comfort of your own couch. It doesn't get much better than that.

HIGHLIGHTS: They have a variety of cookie flavors: anything from the classic Chocolate Chip to White Chocolate Almond.

Need milk with those warm cookies? No problem. They'll deliver milk too.

INSIDER TIPS: If you plan on picking up cookies from their store, call 30 minutes ahead to guarantee the cookies are warm for you.

PHOTOS (LEFT TO RIGHT):
Jennifer Diaz (@jenmdiaz)
Mali Schneiter (@malikathleen)

WRITER: Abby Reuther (@abby.reuther)

LAS PALETAS

OVERVIEW:
What's better than a popsicle on a warm, sunny day? Absolutely nothing! Now picture fresh fruit and herbs embedded into that sweet treat. You're probably drooling, as you should be, because the popsicles are delicious. Las Paletas is a must-stop! They offer a variety of popsicles for every palate, and they're made in-house.

COST: $

ADDRESS: 2911 12th Ave S

NEIGHBORHOOD: 12 South

HOURS: Tues – Sat, 11am – 8pm
Sun – Mon, 11am – 6pm

PHONE: 1.615.386.2101

WEBSITE: laspaletasnashville.com

INSTAGRAM: @laspaletasnashville

COMMUNITY FAVORITE:
Avocado—trust me. It sounds strange, but it's creamy, sweet, and refreshing. Another favorite is Cookies. Just as the name states— it's cookies jam-packed into a popsicle.

PHOTOS (LEFT TO RIGHT):
Angela Ignasky (@angiggy)
Cabell Johnson (@cabellkristine)
Laura Emerson (@Lulu6252)
Roxanne Todor (@roxy_tee)

WRITER:
Sarah Patton (@sarahcharlottepatton)

ATMOSPHERE:
Las Paletas is tucked into the 12 South neighborhood in an all-white chic building. It's an intimate space with minimal seating inside, but there are benches on the front porch and around the outside so the littles can run wild. Most people enjoy their treats on the go and even stroll through Sevier Park or hit up the nearby shops.

HIGHLIGHTS:
They have a couple of different popsicle categories: cream, fruit, and sugar-free.

Feeling a little wild? Get your popsicle chocolate dipped!

It's a place for all ages. You'll find couples, families, and teens strolling in and out of the building during their peak season.

The line moves pretty quickly, and they post their daily menu online.

INSIDER TIPS:
The menu changes every day, and once the flavor is gone, it's gone!

They have chiquita-sized (mini-sized) popsicles for the kiddos, and you can ask for a holder so it doesn't drip down on their hands and clothes. These ladies have thought of it all!

MIKE'S ICE CREAM

OVERVIEW: Famous for their old-fashioned handmade ice cream in 30 different flavors, Mike's also has an old-fashioned soda fountain and a full coffee and espresso bar.

COST: $

ADDRESS: 208 Broadway

NEIGHBORHOOD: Downtown

HOURS: Every day, 8am – midnight

PHONE: 1.615.742.6453

WEBSITE: mikesicecream.com

INSTAGRAM: @mikesicecream

ATMOSPHERE: A small, bright ice cream parlor right in the middle of all the honky tonks on Broadway. It's usually packed with a wide variety of tourists, tipsy honky tonkers, families, and locals that need their dose of handmade ice cream.

HIGHLIGHTS: If you're not a huge fan of ice cream, try one of their old-fashioned fountain sodas, and if you feel a little wild, make it a float! Or maybe a frozen cappuccino is more up your alley. For all those health-conscious folks, they also have soft-serve yogurt that is divine.

INSIDER TIPS: The line is usually to the door or even out the door, but this is normal and the line moves fast so don't let that stop you.

PHOTOS (LEFT TO RIGHT):
Emily Sherman (@emilyysherman) and Ashley Terry (@trashleyterry)

WRITER: Abby Reuther (@abby.reuther)

TEMPERED CAFE & CHOCOLATE

OVERVIEW: This is a cafe specializing in small-batch artisan chocolates, wine and cheese pairings, sandwiches, croissants, and so much more.

COST: $$

ADDRESS: 1201 5th Avenue N

NEIGHBORHOOD: Germantown

HOURS: Tues – Fri, 11am – 7pm
Sat – Sun, 9am – 7pm
The Green Hour (21+): Thur, 8pm – 1am and
Fri – Sat, 8pm – 3am

PHONE: 1.615.454.5432

WEBSITE: temperednashville.com

INSTAGRAM: @temperednashville and @greenhournashville

ATMOSPHERE: You won't feel like you're in Nashville; rather, a small elegant cafe somewhere in Europe. It's quaint and intimate.

HIGHLIGHTS: They make all their truffles in-house. My personal favorites are French Extra Dark (dark), Browned Butter (dark), and Browned Butter Cream (dark). Can you tell I have a love for dark chocolate?

INSIDER TIPS: They host classes in the shop, like a chocolate truffle–making class! Check their website for the schedule.

PHOTOS (LEFT TO RIGHT): Aubrey Hine (@aubreyhine) and Holly Darnell (@hollywood_25)

WRITER: Abby Reuther (@abby.reuther)

EAT + DRINK

bars

12TH SOUTH TAPROOM & GRILL

OVERVIEW: 12th South Taproom & Grill features a large selection of craft beers and made-to-order, delicious pub food.

COST: $$

ADDRESS: 2318 12th Ave S

NEIGHBORHOOD: 12 South

HOURS: Every day, 11am – midnight

PHONE: 1.615.463.7552

WEBSITE: 12southtaproom.com

INSTAGRAM: @12southtaproom

ATMOSPHERE: A casual and laid-back pub with indoor and outdoor seating and that local neighborhood hangout vibe.

HIGHLIGHTS: It's not your typical pub food— it's made-to-order and they use local, organic produce and grass-fed free-range Tennessee beef.

They have a large selection of craft beers. The staff is always very knowledgeable and willing to help you pick the perfect beer for your taste buds.

INSIDER TIPS: Bring your pup and enjoy the patio! Check their events calender online for their live music schedule.

PHOTOS (LEFT TO RIGHT):
Lindsey McPherson (@TheNashvilleMom)
Kendall Rowe (@krowe1088)

WRITER:
Abby Reuther (@abby.reuther)

SANTA'S PUB

OVERVIEW: Santa's Pub is housed in a double-wide trailer. Christmas decor, cheap beer, and karaoke makes it one of Nashville's favorite dive bars.

COST: $

ADDRESS: 2225 Bransford Ave

NEIGHBORHOOD: Wedgewood Houston

HOURS: Every day, 4pm - 2:30am

PHONE: 1.615.593.1872

WEBSITE: santaspub.com

INSTAGRAM: @santaspub

ATMOSPHERE: This isn't a place you need to get dressed up for—it's a smoke-filled karaoke joint.

HIGHLIGHTS: The bar only accepts cash, and beers start at $2.

There's karaoke every night starting at 7pm (9pm on Sundays).

Santa is present most of the time—you can't miss his white beard and jolly grin.

INSIDER TIPS: Celebrities have been known to pop into the trailer and sing some of their own tunes!

PHOTOS (LEFT TO RIGHT):
Eleanor Phillips
Winnie Wong (@wnne_wng)

WRITER:
Sarah Patton (@sarahcharlottepatton)

3 CROW BAR

OVERVIEW: A popular neighborhood bar in the famous Five-Points area that serves great cocktails, beers, and delicious food.

COST: $

ADDRESS: 1024 Woodland St

NEIGHBORHOOD: East Nashville

HOURS: Every day, 11am – 3am

PHONE: 1.615.262.3345

WEBSITE: 3crowbar.com

INSTAGRAM: @3crowbar

ATMOSPHERE: Filled with chill vibes, it's a laid-back bar full of regulars, East Nashville hipsters, and those brave souls who crossed the river to come hang out in the East side. There's a great covered back bar and tree-covered deck.

HIGHLIGHTS: Trivia night is every Thursday at 8pm. Get there early to secure a spot.

2-for-1's are every Sunday from noon until late and again on Wednesday's from 7pm until late.

INSIDER TIPS: If you aren't a fan of smoke, snag a seat in their back patio or by a window inside when they have them open.

Try their Black Bean Burger—it's my favorite.

PHOTOS (LEFT TO RIGHT):
Tieka Ellis (@SelectPotential)
Abby Reuther (@abby.reuther)

WRITER: Abby Reuther (@abby.reuther)

THE CRYING WOLF

OVERVIEW: It's a hip hangout bar perfect for catching a concert in the back room or drinking with friends and making memories.

COST: $

ADDRESS: 823 Woodland St

NEIGHBORHOOD: East Nashville

HOURS: Every day, 5pm – 3am

PHONE: 1.615.953.6715

WEBSITE: thecryingwolf.com

INSTAGRAM: @thecryingwolfbar

ATMOSPHERE: Billiards, a patio, and a smorgasbord of interesting taxidermy make for a unique and perfectly weird hangout spot.

HIGHLIGHTS: Happy hour is Sunday through Thursday, 5 to 8pm, and includes two sliders and a PBR for $6, $2 select beers, $6 double well drinks, and $6 shot + PBR. Every day, all day, $5 well shots.

The food is delicious, especially their burgers. They butcher and grind their beef in-house and all their sauces are also made in-house.

INSIDER TIPS: Get there early and stay for the weirdness. Embrace and love the weirdness. It's Nashville, and The Crying Wolf meets the real people where they want to be.

PHOTOS (LEFT TO RIGHT):
David Fowlkes (@Davidfowlkes) and Matt Vasilogambros (@Mattyvas)

WRITER: Kelley Griggs (@kelleyboothe)

BACK ALLEY DINER

OVERVIEW: It's a downtown diner and bar located in an alley (literally), featuring a comfort-food menu, full bar, and live music.

COST: $

ADDRESS: 217 Arcade Alley

NEIGHBORHOOD: Downtown

HOURS: Mon, 10:30am – 2:30pm
Tues – Thur, 10:30am – 9pm
Fri, 10:30am – 10pm
Sat, 11am – 10pm

PHONE: 1.615.251.3003

WEBSITE: backalleydiner.com

INSTAGRAM: @backalleydiner

ATMOSPHERE: Just what you'd expect from a bar in an alley—a true hidden gem. It has a funky tavern vibe, where regulars are present and newbies are welcome.

HIGHLIGHTS: On Saturday night, they feature live music starting at 7pm, and run specials for 50-cent wings until 10pm and $2 PBRs all night. Happy hour is Tuesday through Friday from 4 to 7pm.

INSIDER TIPS: Parking doesn't really exist. You'll need to park in a nearby paid lot, or better yet grab an Uber or Lyft.

If you work downtown, it's a great lunch break spot to avoid busy Broadway.

PHOTOS (LEFT TO RIGHT):
Abbey Frei (@abbey_frei) and Sarah Patton (@sarahcharlottepatton)

WRITER: Abby Reuther (@abby.reuther)

VILLAGE PUB

OVERVIEW:
Village Pub is a 21+ restaurant and bar located in the heart of Riverside Village in East Nashville. They are known for their mules, beers on draft, and pretzels. Village Pub serves both lunch and dinner with outdoor patio seating available.

COST: $$

ADDRESS: 1308 McGavock Pike

NEIGHBORHOOD: East Nashville

HOURS:
Mon – Thur, 11:30am – midnight
Fri – Sat, 11:30am – 1am

PHONE: 1.615.942.5880

WEBSITE: riversidevillagepub.com

INSTAGRAM: @villagepubandbeergarden

COMMUNITY FAVORITE:
Try the English Ass (gin mule) and Chipotle Black Bean Burger.

PHOTOS (LEFT TO RIGHT):
Abby Reuther (@abby.reuther)
Mali Schneiter (@malikathleen)
Holly Darnell (@hollywood_25)
Aubrey Hine (@aubreyhine)

WRITER:
Holly Darnell (@hollywood_25)

ATMOSPHERE:

It's a smaller pub with a local feel and laid-back atmosphere. They have a great patio that is dog friendly too!

HIGHLIGHTS:

A highlight at Village Pub is Mule Monday, where mules are featured at half-price from 11:30am–10pm on Monday evenings.

The three TVs located throughout the bar make for excellent sports watching, especially during Predators season.

They also have a wide selection of board games available to play.

INSIDER TIPS:

A traditional mule is made with ginger beer, fresh lime, and vodka, and served in a mug. Village Pub steps up the mule game and allows you to personalize it with your liquor of choice including gin, bourbon, vodka, tequila, rum, and scotch. I usually pick the English Ass (the gin mule), but I've tried several of the others and you really can't go wrong.

The giant pretzels are a must-eat, especially when served with local Yazoo beer cheese dip and stone ground mustard. If you're feeling a little hungrier, look no further than the stuffed pretzel sandwiches. My favorites are the Chipotle Black Bean Burger or the Blackened Chicken Sandwich paired with the must-have side of Ruffles potato chips.

DINO'S BAR

OVERVIEW: This is the oldest dive bar in East Nashville, where they say "every hour is happy hour." They specialize in late-night food, cheap beer, and good times.

COST: $

ADDRESS: 411 Gallatin Ave

NEIGHBORHOOD: East Nashville

HOURS: Mon – Fri, 4pm – 3am
Sat – Sun, noon – 3am

PHONE: 1.615.226.3566

WEBSITE: dinosnashville.com

INSTAGRAM: @dinosnashville

ATMOSPHERE: Dino's possesses a true dive bar atmosphere without the smoke-filled bar. For all those smokers out there, don't worry— you can smoke on their back patio.

HIGHLIGHTS: Their Dino's Cheeseburger + Fries is the bomb. Enjoy brunch on Saturday and Sunday from noon to 4pm. It's been a backdrop for photo shoots with celebrities such as Keith Urban.

INSIDER TIPS: Parking is limited. I recommend trying to get a spot on one of the streets around the bar and walking there. Dino's is family friendly until 8pm.

PHOTOS (LEFT TO RIGHT):
Kaitie Moyer (@mccarnbnb) and Micki Windham (@mickiwindham)

WRITER: Abby Reuther (@abby.reuther)

GREENHOUSE BAR

OVERVIEW: It's exactly what it sounds like: a full bar inside a glass greenhouse. It's pretty magical.

COST: $$

ADDRESS: 2211 Bandywood Dr

NEIGHBORHOOD: Green Hills

HOURS: Every day, 4pm – 3am

PHONE: 1.615.385.3357

WEBSITE: thefoodcompanynashville.com

INSTAGRAM: @greenhousebarnashville

ATMOSPHERE: The floors are covered with gravel. The lights are dim and the bar is small. It's laid-back and unique; no frills and close to nature; a greenhouse away from home, if you will. It's a great place for the after-work cocktail with your real friends, the ones you never have to impress.

HIGHLIGHTS: There's cool people, cold beer, hard trivia, good burgers, and green plants—like heaven but on earth.

INSIDER TIPS: If you don't know the bartender Ginger Brad, you are doing it all wrong. When you go, ask for him.

When it rains, the rain hits the glass roof. It's magical and cozy. Next time it rains I recommend getting there fast.

PHOTOS (LEFT TO RIGHT):
Emma Denley (@emmaann13) and Selah Decew (@selahdecew)

WRITER: Kelley Griggs (@kelleyboothe)

LOSERS BAR

OVERVIEW: Part dive bar, part honky tonk, and part popular gathering spot among local singles, Losers is a go-to for drinks, dancing, and good times outside of the usual Broadway scene.

COST: $

ADDRESS: 1911 Division St

NEIGHBORHOOD: Midtown

HOURS: Every day, 11am – 3am

PHONE: 1.615.327.3115

WEBSITE: losersbarnashville.com

INSTAGRAM: @losersbar

ATMOSPHERE: With sister bars Winners and Losers right next to each other, choosing one is hard. Dark and divey, but slightly classier than the honky tonks on Lower Broad, you'll find a mix of people packing out the dance floor and large wooden patio at Losers.

HIGHLIGHTS: There's a band every Friday and Saturday night playing country and rock covers, plus multiple events throughout the week where you can catch local live music.

INSIDER TIPS: Whiskey Jam, a free concert hosted by sister restaurant Winners every Monday night, features some big names in music plus plenty of surprise celebrity guests.

PHOTOS (LEFT TO RIGHT):
Katie Garfield (@katie.garfield)
Teresa S. (@teresamariaaa)

WRITER: Kristen Shoates (@kristennicole86)

THE CENTENNIAL

OVERVIEW: This is a dive bar that's simple and classic. It is a wonderful, casual, and treasured bar among the Nashville bar scene.

COST: $

ADDRESS: 5115 Centennial Blvd

NEIGHBORHOOD: The Nations

HOURS: Sun – Thur, 11am – 1pm
Fri – Sat, 11am – 3am

PHONE: 1.615.679.9746

WEBSITE: centennialnashville.com

INSTAGRAM: @centennial_nash

ATMOSPHERE: The Centennial has the perfect neighborhood bar atmosphere. It's a true dive bar with a casual, laid-back interior and dim lighting. There's also a great outdoor yard with covered and uncovered areas. They have cornhole!

HIGHLIGHTS: The food is good! They even offer pretzels buns, and who doesn't love a pretzel bun?! Try their Cauliflower Tacos and Prime Dip.

They serve beer AND liquor. Their local beer selection is on-point too.

INSIDER TIPS: The owner is super friendly and always there. He is usually serving the drinks, so be nice and courteous.

PHOTOS (LEFT TO RIGHT):
Abby Reuther (@abby.reuther) and Holly Darnell (@hollywood_25)

WRITER: Allison Holley (@appleandoaknash)

TWO BITS

OVERVIEW:
This is not your typical bar. There's great food and cocktails, and lots of FREE games. You'll go for one drink and end up staying all night. It's the perfect place to let your inner child out while making memories with family and friends.

COST: $

ADDRESS: 1520 Demonbreun St

NEIGHBORHOOD: Demonbreun Hill

HOURS: Sun – Wed, 11am – 11pm
Thur – Sat, 11am – 3am

WEBSITE: twobitsnashville.com

INSTAGRAM: @twobitsnash

COMMUNITY FAVORITE:
For brunch, try the Grit Idea (housemade bacon, jalapeño-spiked cheese grits, honey sourdough toast, and two sunny-side-up eggs). Drink the Honey Boo Boo Bear (Jack Daniels Honey, lemon juice, simple syrup, and lemonade). Spiced Bacon Popcorn is a fantastic snack or appetizer, and Carnitas Tacos (avocado crema, onion, cilantro, jalapeño, and pineapple) make a great lunch or dinner.

PHOTOS (LEFT TO RIGHT):
Ashley Hylbert (@Whiteavestudio)
Marilyn Lauterbach (@NashvilleFoodAuthority)
Katie Roth (@kroth17)
Sarah Patton (@sarahcharlottepatton)

WRITER:
Abby Reuther (@abby.reuther)

ATMOSPHERE:

Of the popular bars on busy Demonbreun Street, Two Bits stands out with its bright signage and patio, often with people playing a giant game of Connect Four or Jenga.

The interior of Two Bits is welcoming, with exposed brick walls, leather U-shaped booths, high-top tables, and classic arcade games.

It's the perfect place to hang out and play some friendly competitive games with friends. It's also a great date spot–take the awkwardness out of first dates by grabbing some drinks and playing a classic game of Connect Four (Hint: men, let the ladies win).

HIGHLIGHTS:

The highlights, first and foremost, are the games (duh)! Leave your quarters at home because all the games are FREE and they have a variety of board games, classic arcade games, TV games (Nintendo), shuffleboard, and many more.

The menu is unique, eclectic, and fun just like their atmosphere.

There are 24 draft beers each night and half of them are local brews–YAY to supporting local! They also have a fantastic cocktail menu made from fresh ingredients. My personal favorite is the Honey Boo Boo Bear– saying the name is half the fun.

INSIDER TIPS:

There's really no parking besides a few spots on the street out front. I'd highly recommend getting an Uber or Lyft, so that way you can stay for "just one more."

OLD GLORY

OVERVIEW: A renovated 1920s boiler room now dedicated to cocktails, food, and fun times. Drinking a cocktail here blows your mind on all levels.

COST: $$

ADDRESS: 1200 Villa Pl #103

NEIGHBORHOOD: Edgehill Village

HOURS: Sun – Thur, noon – 1am
Fri – Sat, noon – 2am

PHONE: 1.615.679.0509

WEBSITE: facebook.com/oldglorynashville/

INSTAGRAM: @oldglorynashville

ATMOSPHERE: It's impossible for a renovated 60-foot high, 1920s boiler room to not have a unique atmosphere. What stories could these walls tell?

HIGHLIGHTS: One highlight is that you get to enjoy three different levels, with two levels looking down on the main floor and cocktail-making action.

INSIDER TIPS: It's hard to find. Making the entrance to this bar unadvertised and low key only adds to the experience. The entrance can be found in an alleyway behind the shops of Edgehill Village. Its door is only recognizable by the yellow/gold triangle that is painted around it. This makes for a secretive and hidden gem.

PHOTOS (LEFT TO RIGHT):
Malo-Lennon Simmermon (@mallorylennonmusic)
Margaret, M. (@livin4eaternity)

WRITER: Joe Beecroft (@thelocalperspective)

ROBERT'S WESTERN WORLD

OVERVIEW: This is the best little honky tonk on Broadway, known for playing traditional country. Robert's is a local and tourist favorite.

COST: $

ADDRESS: 416 Broadway

NEIGHBORHOOD: Downtown

HOURS: Mon – Sat, 11am – 3am
Sun, noon – 3am

PHONE: 1.615.244.9552

WEBSITE: robertswesternworld.com

INSTAGRAM: @robertswesternworld

ATMOSPHERE: The walls are lined with boots and neon. You will walk in to traditional country music and usually a few couples two-stepping. It is a refreshing step back in time.

HIGHLIGHTS: The Fried Bologna Sandwich is pretty much the best thing you will ever put in your mouth—other than their Grilled Cheese.

INSIDER TIPS: All ages are welcome until 6pm; after that 21 and up only. The owner is also a member of the house band, so watch your manners. Also, I hear you can have your wedding here! Make all your hillbilly dreams come true right here in Nashville.

PHOTOS (LEFT TO RIGHT):
Kelly Mandeville (@devillainess)
Abby Reuther (@abby.reuther)

WRITER: Allison Holley (@appleandoaknash)

ACME FEED & SEED

OVERVIEW:
Located on lower Broadway, Acme Feed & Seed is a modern take on the classic honky tonk. There are four floors of fun, with live music, cold drinks, Southern cuisine, sushi, and a killer rooftop bar.

COST: $$

ADDRESS: 101 Broadway

NEIGHBORHOOD: Downtown

HOURS: Mon – Fri, 11am – close
Sat – Sun, 10am – close

PHONE: 1.615.915.0888

WEBSITE: theacmenashville.com

INSTAGRAM: @acmenashville

COMMUNITY FAVORITE:
The rooftop bar, dancing (not in a line), and the Mule Kicker (an adult slushie) are worth experiencing.

PHOTOS (LEFT TO RIGHT):
Welsey Fitzhugh (@welseyf)
Sarah Graif (@sarahgraif)
Danielle Burton (@dburts)
Ali Landry (@Ali__landry)

WRITER:
Allison Holley (@appleandoaknash)

ATMOSPHERE:

Acme is a new twist on the classic honky tonk. The first floor has more of the classic honky-tonk feel with live music and Southern cuisine. The second floor has more of a sports-bar feel, but with a sushi bar in the back. The third floor is a private event space called The Hatchery, which sometimes houses intimate concerts. The fourth floor is the rooftop bar! Each floor offers something different and it's the reason why it's one of my favorite bars downtown.

HIGHLIGHTS:

The rooftop often has great local DJs for a nice break from the county music scene. I also believe the rooftop has the best view of downtown and it looks over the Cumberland River and popular pedestrian bridge too.

The sushi is AMAZING. I personally think it's Nashville's best sushi.

INSIDER TIPS:

There are many (cool and clean) bathrooms located in the basement. There is only one on the rooftop, so plan accordingly.

If you like a little spice, try the Zydeco (a drink shared with their sister property, The Southern Steak & Oyster).

The entry line can be pretty long, so go early on weekends.

If you want a place to dance and need a break from Wagon Wheel and Luke Bryan covers, head on down to Acme Feed & Seed.

EAT + DRINK

breweries
+ distilleries

CORSAIR BREWSTILLERY

OVERVIEW: Widely known for their whiskey, Corsair also distills gin, vodka, rye whiskey, and seasonal and experimental liquors. They make beer too, which is only available at the Brewstillery for now.

COST: $$

ADDRESS: 1200 Clinton St #110
For their other location, please visit the website.

NEIGHBORHOOD: Marathon Village

HOURS: Tues – Fri, 11am – 8pm
Sat, noon – 7pm
Sun, noon – 6pm

PHONE: 1.615.200.0320

WEBSITE: corsairdistillery.com

INSTAGRAM: @corsairdistillery

ATMOSPHERE: Located in Marathon Village, Corsair has an old-school, charming feel. The facility has exposed brick and dim lighting with an outdoor patio perfect for cocktail sipping.

HIGHLIGHTS: They have a taproom where you can grab a Corsair beer to enjoy on your tour or simply enjoy at the bar or back patio.

INSIDER TIPS: Daily tours fill up fast, so I recommend booking at least 2 weeks in advance, especially if you have a larger group of people and want a tour on a weekend.

PHOTOS (LEFT TO RIGHT):
Elly Deutch (@EllyDeutch) and Jackie Wall (@jackierwall)

WRITER: Holly Darnell (@hollywood_25)

FAT BOTTOM

OVERVIEW:
One of Nashville's beloved local breweries, Fat Bottom was originally located on the East Side, but due to tremendous success, recently expanded to the West Side. The bitter smell of homegrown hops seeps from the boiler room to the bar and into the yard. The menu boasts a wide selection of food and beer for the fast-casual connoisseur. Or–you could stay a while and have another.

COST: $$

ADDRESS: 800 44th Avenue N

NEIGHBORHOOD: The Nations

HOURS: Every day, 11am – midnight

PHONE: 1.615.678.5715

WEBSITE: fatbottombrewing.com

INSTAGRAM: @fatbottombrews

COMMUNITY FAVORITE:
The Ruby Red is my beer of choice. Don't forget to try their seasonal beers, like the Ginger.

PHOTOS (LEFT TO RIGHT):
Corey R Hargis (@corehyargis)
Jessica C. (@JessIsLiving)
Abby Reuther (@abby.reuther)
Nikki Johnson (@justinjohnsonlive)

WRITER:
Kelley Griggs (@kelleyboothe)

ATMOSPHERE:

The aesthetic of the place screams Nashville—large wooden tables, brick walls, concrete floors, and wood-plated accent walls. It's a large space with plenty of room—great for large groups, an all-day hangout spot, after-work drink, and dinner spot.

HIGHLIGHTS:

They say it best: "We set out to make beers that are bigger and sexier than what you can find at your local bar." Are you hooked yet? Each brew batch is brewed from the highest quality ingredients and perfected each time.

Although their beer is the center of attention, as it should be, they also have a great menu of seasonal salads, burgers, vegetarian options, plated meals, and shareable plates that will have you licking your lips and wanting more.

Want to take some brews home with you? They have you covered with their beer filling station.

INSIDER TIPS:

Need a private event space? They have a private room called The Reserve that can be rented out and can seat 150 to 200 people.

Bring your out-of-town friends here. It's a subtle way to let them know up-front that you are a beer snob and you aren't messing around about knowing all the decent spots.

BEARDED IRIS BREWING

OVERVIEW: It's a brewery taproom offering six beers on tap with rotating specialty beer.

COST: $

ADDRESS: 101 Van Buren St

NEIGHBORHOOD: Germantown

HOURS: Tues – Thur, 5 – 10pm
Fri, 5 – 11pm
Sat, noon – 11pm
Sun, noon – 8pm

PHONE: 1.615.928.7988

WEBSITE: beardedirisbrewing.com

INSTAGRAM: @beardediris

ATMOSPHERE: Chandeliers hang from the ceiling and the taproom floor is made of black and white checkerboard. Antique couches, round tables, and barstools make it a great place to meet up with some friends, hang out, and enjoy some local beer.

HIGHLIGHTS: The taproom is kid friendly! Beer flights are not available for purchase, but they will allow you to sample any beer.

INSIDER TIPS: When hunger strikes, you can purchase food from a local food truck parked outside. You can also bring your own food.

PHOTOS (LEFT TO RIGHT):
Brittni (@iphonetourist) and Rachel Ciarletta (@ciao_bella1038)

WRITER:
Holly Darnell (@hollywood_25)

YAZOO BREWING COMPANY

OVERVIEW: The brewery that established craft beer in Nashville, pronounced YEAH-Zoo if you're a local.

COST: $

ADDRESS: 910 Division St

NEIGHBORHOOD: The Gulch

HOURS: Wed – Thur, 3 – 9pm
Fri, 2 – 9pm
Sat, 11am – 9pm

PHONE: 1.615.891.4649

WEBSITE: yazoobrew.com

INSTAGRAM: @yazoobrew + @yazootaproom

ATMOSPHERE: There's a casual and loud crowd. The taproom and tours are popular hangs on Thursday nights and the weekends. The partially covered patio is a great place to taste a flight of beer too.

HIGHLIGHTS: Favorites include the Hefeweizen (it tastes like banana, in a good way), the Dos Perros, and the Sly Rye Porter. You'll find these around town, but there are also some seasonal brews only available here.

INSIDER TIPS: The brew tour is a must. If you like sour beer, they often have 3 or 4 options in the summer. Sometimes there's a food truck out front.

PHOTOS (LEFT TO RIGHT):
Ashley (@downbydubay) and Russ Phillips (@dafad36)

WRITER: Alex Tapper (@fantasticmrtapp)

TENNESSEE BREW WORKS

OVERVIEW:
It's obviously a brewery, but just because they're beer fanatics, they didn't skimp in the design department. It's a go-to spot when the weather is spectacular, and my most recommended brewery. Their staff is friendly and makes you feel like you've known them forever. It's great for date night or big groups, and you can make it a daytime pit stop or low-key night out.

COST: $$

ADDRESS: 809 Ewing Ave

NEIGHBORHOOD: The Gulch

HOURS: Mon – Fri, 5 – 10pm
Sat, noon – 10pm
Sun, 11am – 8pm

PHONE: 1.615.436.0050

WEBSITE: tnbrew.com

INSTAGRAM: @tnbrewworks

COMMUNITY FAVORITE:
Southern Wit is my go-to beer, and if you're ordering from the kitchen, don't overlook the Baja Fish Tacos or Five Beer Burger.

PHOTOS (LEFT TO RIGHT):
Kate Wilke (@kateewilke)
Leslie Reynolds (@lesterva)
Justin Willenbrink (@kegpeddler)
Keira LeFranc (@sovinteresting)

WRITER: Sarah Patton (@sarahcharlottepatton)

ATMOSPHERE:

Hands down, it's the best looking brewery in town. They have one of the largest taprooms (with two bars!!) in Nashville and there's plenty of seating for everyone. It's open and spacious so everyone feels like they're right where the beer-making happens.

Their patio is to die for. With a large upper and lower patio, there's enough space for everyone. Enjoy the views of downtown, sip on a beer or two, and enjoy good times with friends.

And did I mention, TWO bars?!

HIGHLIGHTS:

They have live music Wednesday through Saturday and spin records on Sunday. Wednesday is known as "brew-for-one"—you can get two pints for the price of one.

Many bars and restaurants around town serve their beers—M.L. Rose, Adele's, Neighbors of Sylvan Park, Acme Feed & Seed, The Flipside, Martin's BBQ, and many more, so be sure to keep an eye out for them.

INSIDER TIPS:

Get a flight of beer and try them all.

They're dog friendly, so grab the pooch.

If you love events (like me), they're a great space to host a party.

Check their calendar on their website for special events and live music performances.

SOUTHERN GRIST BREWING COMPANY

OVERVIEW: This is a locally owned and operated microbrewery and taproom.

COST: $

ADDRESS: 1201 Porter Rd

NEIGHBORHOOD: East Nashville

HOURS: Tues – Thur, 4 – 10pm
Fri, 4 – 11pm
Sat, noon – 11pm
Sun, noon – 8pm

PHONE: 1.615.727.1201

WEBSITE: southerngristbrewing.com

INSTAGRAM: @southerngristbrewing

ATMOSPHERE: It's a casual neighborhood brewery with friendly and knowledgeable staff.

HIGHLIGHTS: They have a tasty variety of rotating craft brews they brew in-house. The brewer masters are the owners. Oh, and the soft pretzels with beer cheese are amazing.

INSIDER TIPS: You can order from their menu or they allow outside delivery.
The pretzels are more like fluffy, buttery breadsticks, but they are SO GOOD. They allow you to sample beer before you commit and they offer flights. They also sell crowlers (can growlers) if you'd like to get your favorites to go! Dogs are allowed outside.

PHOTOS (LEFT TO RIGHT):
Michelle Tibbs (@michellemary88) and Rachael Raffle (@raelynn_3)

WRITER: Allison Holley (@appleandoaknash)

NELSON'S GREEN BIER DISTILLERY

OVERVIEW: It's a family-owned whiskey business with tours and tastings and a gift shop for all your whiskey needs.

COST: $$

ADDRESS: 1414 Clinton St

NEIGHBORHOOD: Marathon Village

HOURS:
Tours and Tasting:
Mon, 11am – 5pm every hour
Tues – Sat, 11am – 6pm every half hour
Sun, 11am – 5pm every half hour

Gift Shop:
Tues – Sat, 11am – 7pm
Sun – Mon, 11am – 6pm

PHONE: 1.615.913.8800

WEBSITE: greenbrierdistillery.com

INSTAGRAM: @tnwhiskeyco

ATMOSPHERE: Exposed brick walls, dim lighting, bourbon barrels—what more could you want while sipping whiskey? They also offer an event rental space called The Oak Room.

HIGHLIGHTS: There's a great family story behind how this Nashville distillery started. Make sure to check it out on their website.

INSIDER TIPS: It's highly recommended to book your tour online in advance.

PHOTOS (LEFT TO RIGHT):
Memorie White (@Memorieesq) and Holly Darnell (@hollywood_25)

WRITER: Abby Reuther (@abby.reuther)

EAT + DRINK

markets

SOUTHERNAIRE MARKET

OVERVIEW: This downtown market has local food, produce, fresh meat, seafood, made-to-order paninis, craft beer, and coffee.

COST: $$

ADDRESS: 150 3rd Ave S

NEIGHBORHOOD: Sobro

HOURS: Mon – Sat, 10am – 5:30pm
Sun, noon – 5:30pm

PHONE: 1.615.490.8077

WEBSITE: southernairemarket.com

INSTAGRAM: @southernairemarket

ATMOSPHERE: It's located in the Pinnacle Building and is next door to its sister property, The Southern Steak & Oyster. It encompasses the style of a New Orleans-style neighborhood grocery and is filled with that Southern hospitality.

HIGHLIGHTS: It's the perfect market for getting groceries or just grabbing a quick snack or lunch to go.

INSIDER TIPS: If you can't make it to the market, they have delivery options on their website.

PHOTOS (LEFT TO RIGHT):
Caitlin Bloodworth (@Caitlin_Bloodworth)
Eliza Kennard Photography (@elizakennard)

WRITER: Abby Reuther (@abby.reuther)

PORTER ROAD BUTCHER

OVERVIEW:
Porter Road Butcher's meat is locally sourced and kindly, humanely, and pasture raised. When you ask Chris, one of PRB's owners, why he and James started Porter Road, he'll tell you succinctly that "It's the only way to do it." I shop at PRB because I know that I'm supporting a meat industry that I believe in.

COST: $$

ADDRESS: 501 Gallatin Ave

NEIGHBORHOOD: East Nashville

HOURS: Mon - Fri, 11am - 7pm
Sat, 10am - 6pm

WEBSITE: prbutcher.com

INSTAGRAM: @prbutcher

COMMUNITY FAVORITE:
There's bacon, bacon, and more bacon.

The sausages are delicious—made with fresh herbs and quality meat (no mystery meat!).

PHOTOS (LEFT TO RIGHT):
Abby Reuther (@abby.reuther)
Holly Darnell (@hollywood_25)
Abby Reuther (@abby.reuther)
Sarah Patton (@sarahcharlottepatton)

WRITER:
Kate Moore (@moore_kate)

ATMOSPHERE:

They pride themselves on being the neighborhood shop, meaning they know their customers by name and are always happy to take the time to chat and offer advice. They always know the answers to my questions.

HIGHLIGHTS:

In addition to cuts of meat, they have a broad selection of sausages, jerky, prepared foods, cheese, charcuterie, fresh bread, and local jams and pickles.

Everything at PRB screams local. They don't carry "fresh" chicken when chicken is not in season. Did you know that chickens even have a season?! These people are experts.

Also, have they baked anything today? ASK! And then order that. These people aren't just meat people—they're chefs. They know what goodness tastes like and they pride themselves on providing that.

INSIDER TIPS:

Ask questions. Be open. Try something new! Give them a budget and let them go from there.

Let them provide all of the ingredients for you. You'll notice that they have a few coolers and shelves equipped with housemade stocks, spices, and sauces and also local cheeses, butters, and soaps!

It never hurts to call ahead if you're looking for something specific.

NASHVILLE FARMER'S MARKET

OVERVIEW:
This year-round, indoor and outdoor fresh market has over 100 local farmers, food stands, street vendors, pop-up shops, vendors, botanists, bakers, and other maker-based artisans.

COST: $

ADDRESS: 900 Rosa L Parks Blvd

NEIGHBORHOOD: Downtown

HOURS:
Farm shed: Every day, 8am – 6pm
Individual farmer days/hours may vary.

Market house restaurants and shops:
Individual shop and restaurant days/hours may vary. Please visit their website for current hours.

PHONE: 1.615.880.2001

WEBSITE: nashvillefarmersmarket.org

INSTAGRAM: @nashvillefarmersmarket

COMMUNITY FAVORITE:
Their Night Market event is a unique experience that includes live music, seasonal cocktails, wine, and craft beer.

PHOTOS (LEFT TO RIGHT):
Kady Alford (@kadyelizabeth)
Elizabeth Merritt (@ms_patria)
Kayla Wagner (@kaylawagner)
Kathleen Clipper (@thenewgirlinnashville)

WRITER:
Kelley Griggs (@kelleyboothe)

ATMOSPHERE:

It's your typical farmer's market atmosphere—casual and laid back. The inside market is spacious with lots of seating.

HIGHLIGHTS:

At the outdoor farm sheds, shoppers have access to a wide variety of seasonal organic fruits, vegetables, meats, spices, herbs, and plants.

The indoor market house is home to a mecca of mouth-watering meals from food stands and street vendors, each representing a culinary experience rooted in Jamaican, Middle Eastern, Mexican, Asian, Indian, Italian, Greek, and American cuisine. It's also home to Shreeji's International Market, The Gardens of Babylon, The Picnic Tap (Craft Brew), and Batch, a shop that sells specialty foods and products local to Nashville.

Sign up for a CSA. Farmers have their individual CSA programs available at their tables. You can also sign up for grower alerts, which I've found really helpful when planning meals.

There are several events at the Farmer's Market that you don't want to miss. Check the event calendar for workshops and gatherings.

INSIDER TIPS:

Bring cash. Most vendors now have credit card machines or readers, but especially during busy times, it's easier. Vendors also tend to appreciate it more since there isn't a surcharge for them. It's also helpful to bring your own bag or basket. It can be a hassle to carry lots of plastic bags.

HEY ROOSTER

OVERVIEW: This general store with a modern twist sells fine handmade goods and small-batch foods by talented makers and craftsmen.

COST: $$

ADDRESS: 1711 21st Ave S

NEIGHBORHOOD: Hillsboro Village

HOURS: Mon – Sat, 10am – 6pm
Sun, 10am – 4pm

WEBSITE: heyrooster.com

INSTAGRAM: @heyrooster

ATMOSPHERE: Hey Rooster might be located in the middle of the busy Hillsboro Village and surrounded by modern shops, but this shop stays true to its roots with an exposed brick wall, brightly colored floor, and an old vintage fridge. Local gifts and handmade goods line the shop, representing a real pride for their home town.

HIGHLIGHTS: There are lots of local goods—a great way to support the local maker and artisan community. You can often find a Matchless Coffee cart parked out front, selling their famous Coffee Soda.

INSIDER TIPS: Since it's in the heart of Hillsboro Village, I suggest making a day or afternoon out of it and exploring the whole neighborhood.

PHOTOS (LEFT TO RIGHT):
Abby Reuther (@abby.reuther)
Lesley Goldrich (@lesgoldrich)

WRITER: Abby Reuther (@abby.reuther)

IMPECCABLE PIG

OVERVIEW: This high-end, trendy boutique has a name that speaks for itself, and each piece you find inside is also statement-worthy.

COST: $$

ADDRESS: 1802 21st Ave S

NEIGHBORHOOD: Hillsboro Village

HOURS: Mon – Sat, 10am – 6pm
Sun, 11am – 5pm

PHONE: 1.615.292.2316

WEBSITE: theimpeccablepig.com

INSTAGRAM: @theimpeccablepig

ATMOSPHERE: While the square footage isn't huge, the store is whitewashed from ceiling to floor—it's uber chic. The music is lively and upbeat.

HIGHLIGHTS: The store is packed with amazing finds from dresses to bags to jewelry. You can walk out with a new ensemble from head to toe or find a piece your closet can't live without.

INSIDER TIPS: It's the perfect spot to snag a date-night outfit or cute shirt for brunch with the girls. My favorite item from Impeccable Pig is a wide-brim charcoal hat. I've received more compliments on this headgear than I can even count.

PHOTOS (LEFT TO RIGHT):
Mali Schneiter (@malikathleen)
Aubrey Hine (@aubreyhine)

WRITER: Sarah Patton (@sarahcharlottepatton)

APPLE & OAK

OVERVIEW: This shop is known for its large selection of rugs, unique vintage furniture, home decor, and small gifts.

COST: $$

ADDRESS: 717 Porter Rd

NEIGHBORHOOD: East Nashville

HOURS: Tues - Fri, 11am - 6pm
Sat - Mon, 12 - 4pm

WEBSITE: appleandoaknash.com

INSTAGRAM: @appleandoaknash

ATMOSPHERE: The walls are filled with home decor and art. It's small and cozy. The owner, Allison, will always make you feel at home and help you find the perfect piece!

HIGHLIGHTS: They have a wide variety of merchandise—greeting cards, bar carts, pillows, wall art, kitchen accessories, rugs, furniture, and much more.

They try and carry as much local merchandise as possible to support local artisans, such as Branded Collective, Love and Lion, and 1767 Designs.

A portion of the sales go to help design local Nashville classrooms—I love that!

INSIDER TIPS: The shop is located in the Shops at Porter East, which has a bunch of other adorable shops—stop by them all!

PHOTOS (LEFT TO RIGHT):
Abby Reuther (@abby.reuther)
Allison Holley (@appleandoaknash)

WRITER: Abby Reuther (@abby.reuther)

WELCOME HOME

OVERVIEW: At Welcome Home, you'll find home decor items like rugs, pillows, art work, lamps, plants, and kitchen items, as well as the perfect gift items for a special someone.

COST: $$

ADDRESS: 1882 Eastland Ave

NEIGHBORHOOD: East Nashville

HOURS: Tues – Sat, 10am – 7pm
Sun, 12 – 5pm

PHONE: 1.615.750.3354

WEBSITE: welcomehomeshop.net

INSTAGRAM: @welcomehomeshop

ATMOSPHERE: Its name says it all. It's a small shop that makes you feel right at home. It's bright and colorful with covered shelves and walls and a whole lot to look at.

HIGHLIGHTS: They really do have the perfect gift selection for anyone. I've gone there countless times looking for gifts without a clue what to buy and I always seem to leave with the perfect gift.

They have a great selection from local artisans and makers. I love their local book selection.

INSIDER TIPS: Ugly Mugs Coffee & Tea is right next door—grab a coffee to go and shop!

PHOTOS (LEFT TO RIGHT):
Silbia Ro (@Silbiaro)
Mali Schneiter (@malikathleen)

WRITER: Abby Reuther (@abby.reuther)

ABSOLUTION

OVERVIEW: This is a unique selection of furniture, home decor, candles, books, jewelry, and many other gifts.

COST: $$$

ADDRESS: The Mall at Green Hills
2126 Abbott Martin Rd #146

NEIGHBORHOOD: Green Hills

HOURS: Mon – Fri, 10am – 9pm

SUN, NOON – 6PM

PHONE: 1.615.515.8442

WEBSITE: seekabsolution.com

INSTAGRAM: @seekabsolution

ATMOSPHERE: Don't panic when you see it's located in the Mall at Green Hills; it's not your typical "mall store." Its interior is more like a charming shop you'd find on a small town Main Street.

HIGHLIGHTS: The shop is filled with fun, unexpected, one-of-a-kind items that will keep you coming back; the perfect mix of antiques and new. Pick out a gift for a friend or treat yourself—you won't regret it (I'm currently drooling over their jewelry).

INSIDER TIPS: With a wide range of items and price points, it's the perfect shop for everyone.

PHOTOS (LEFT TO RIGHT):
Holly Darnell (@hollywood_25)
Abby Reuther (@abby.reuther)

WRITER: Abby Reuther (@abby.reuther)

FABU

OVERVIEW: This shop features women's clothing and accessories, gifts, home decor, and so much more.

COST: $$

ADDRESS: 4606 Charlotte Pike

NEIGHBORHOOD: The Nations

HOURS: Mon – Sat, 10am – 6pm
Sun, 1 – 5pm

PHONE: 1.615.383.0505

WEBSITE: shopfabu.com

INSTAGRAM: @fabunashville

ATMOSPHERE: Located in a historic Victorian house, this shop has 10 rooms (I repeat, 10 rooms) filled with everything you've ever needed and wanted.

Their service is top-notch and will help you find the perfect gift for yourself or someone special.

HIGHLIGHTS: FABU was named "Best Place for a Special Find" by Nashville's Home and Garden magazine—so it's a must-visit shop.

INSIDER TIPS: Take your time going from room to room in the shop because there is so much to see and you don't want to miss any of their treasures.

PHOTOS (LEFT TO RIGHT):
Abby Reuther (@abby.reuther)
Sarah Patton (@sarahcharlottepatton)

WRITER: Abby Reuther (@abby.reuther)

NISOLO

OVERVIEW:
This is the choice purveyor of quality, stylish shoes for the conscious consumer. Roughly, *ni solo* means "not alone" in Spanish. Shopping here helps employ artisan cobblers in Peru and jewelers in Kenya. Nisolo weaves designer silhouettes into heritage craftsmanship, bringing a much-desired local source of timeless essentials. Expect to find your new everyday favorite.

COST: $$$

ADDRESS: 1803 9th Ave N

NEIGHBORHOOD: Buchannan Arts District

HOURS: Mon - Fri, 9am - 6pm
Sat, 11am - 5pm
Sun, 1 - 5pm

PHONE: 1.615.953.1087

WEBSITE: nisolo.com

INSTAGRAM: @nisoloshoes

COMMUNITY FAVORITE:
Men should try Emilio LE and Lockwood, while ladies should look at Austin, Smoking Shoe, and Oliver Oxford.

PHOTOS (LEFT TO RIGHT):
Allison Porterfield (@allison_port)
Abby Reuther (@abby.reuther)
Danielle Luecht (@daniluecht)
Riley Carroll (@orileyaaron)

WRITER:
Alex Tapper (@fantasticmrtapp)

ATMOSPHERE:
This light-filled, minimalist showroom displays men's and women's leather shoes designed in LA, built in Peru, and headquartered in Nashville.

HIGHLIGHTS:
Men, need an everyday boot? These are stiff at first, but will stretch to your foot over time. Leather soles are more formal, rubber more comfortable.

Ladies, indulge in something timeless and sophisticated, yet comfortable and modern. These unique silhouettes get noticed without begging for attention.

The jewelry collections are well-conceived, durable, and affordable.

INSIDER TIPS:
Sometime in mid-summer (usually July), Nisolo will clear old stock with a sale. This is a good time to find a new pair of boots, even if you won't wear them until winter arrives 6 months later. They run out of the good stuff quickly, so keep an eye on their Instagram, and make sure you arrive early.

For some style inspiration, check out their collaborations with local musicians, artists, photographers, and other creatives. Nashvillians will recognize the up-and-coming creatives they feature, and the shoot locations.

Leather soles are soft but their life can be extended with a sole saver—ask your local cobbler. With good care, you could get two or three soles from one pair.

PETER NAPPI

OVERVIEW: This Italian leather footwear and goods store embodies a distinctive Italian heritage combined with an American personality. They carry both men's and woman's products and it's a must-visit!

COST: $$$

ADDRESS: 1308 Adams St
For their other location, please visit the website.

NEIGHBORHOOD: Germantown

HOURS: Mon – Sat, 11am – 6pm
Sun, 12 – 3pm

PHONE: 1.615.248.3310

WEBSITE: peternappi.com

INSTAGRAM: @peternappi

ATMOSPHERE: Housed in a 1900s slaughter house, their space is one of the most gorgeous industrial renovations.

HIGHLIGHTS: Their customer service is second to none and their superior product is recognizable the moment you try it on.

They also sell trinkets and furniture that they find on their European travels.

You can enjoy a cold Peroni or crisp glass of wine as you shop.

INSIDER TIPS: They have four to five parties a year and they always have fantastic live music and Italian food. Check their website for events.

PHOTOS: Gabby Watson (@gbbywtsn + @peternappi)

WRITER: Joe Beecroft (@thelocalperspective)

WILDER

OVERVIEW: From abstract lighting to uniquely crafted jewelry, you're sure to find the perfect item for your home or the perfect gift.

COST: $$$

ADDRESS: 1212 4th Ave N

NEIGHBORHOOD: Germantown

HOURS: Mon – Sat, 11am – 6pm
Sun, noon – 5pm

PHONE: 1.615.679.0008

WEBSITE: wilderlife.com

INSTAGRAM: @wildershop

ATMOSPHERE: Filled with unique items that are created by well-known and not-so-well-known designers, it's as much of an art gallery as it's a store.

HIGHLIGHTS: They have continued collaborations, fantastic parties, and studio visits. The studio visits are a feature on their website. The owners travel to unique studios and sit down with some fascinating people—designers, florists, and ceramic artists, to name a few. It's great to see that they get the inside info on such great curators around America.

INSIDER TIPS: Sign up for the email list to gain access to their website updates and parties.

PHOTOS (LEFT TO RIGHT):
Alex Rosenhaus (@alexdrewandnoone)
Abby Reuther (@abby.reuther)

WRITER: Joe Beecroft (@thelocalperspective)

WHITE'S MERCANTILE

OVERVIEW:
This quaint little shop is located in the heart of 12 South and most recently, downtown Franklin. The rustic general store is stocked floor to ceiling with local home goods, one of a kind jewelry pieces, vintage finds, and exquisite gifts for the whole crew. You'll find a reason to take a piece of Music City home with you.

COST: $$

ADDRESS: 2908 12th Ave S

NEIGHBORHOOD: 12 South

HOURS: Mon – Sat, 10am – 6pm
Sun, noon – 5pm

PHONE: 1.615.750.5379

WEBSITE: whitesmercantile.com

INSTAGRAM: @whitesmercantile

COMMUNITY FAVORITE:
Favorites here include FASHIONABLE leather goods, High Fancy Paper goods, and Becoming jewelry

PHOTOS (LEFT TO RIGHT):
Jennifer Tutor (@alifestyled)
Hollis Dixon (@hollis_dixon)
Darren Jackson (@darren2112)
Darren Jackson (@darren2112)

WRITER:
Aubrey Hine (@aubreyhine)

ATMOSPHERE:

The moment you walk into White's Mercantile, you feel right at home. Old wood floors welcome traveling souls as the fragrant scents of leather, patchouli, and amber from locally poured candles slowly draw you in to every inch of the shop. The open floor plan brilliantly displays both eclectic and functional items along the walls, shelves, and display cases.

HIGHLIGHTS:

If you're looking for a unique gift, a few pieces to tie a room together, or a simple "you deserve this" piece for yourself, look no further. White's Mercantile is your one-stop shop for everything you may need and much more. Not only are their goods locally made, but a large number of items support a good cause. FASHIONABLE, a line of leather totes, wallets, and accessories, helps create jobs for women who are living in poverty. I use my tote for work as a laptop bag, for groceries, hauling gym clothes, or as a hold-all on a night out with friends. Another favorite is the hand-crafted jewelry by Becoming—just another one of the abounding accessories locals swoon over.

INSIDER TIPS:

Shopping local is one of the many gifts Nashville has to offer. Last-minute gifts come easy and affordable and if you're lucky, you just might stop in when a local vendor sets up (a pop-up) shop at either of the two lovely locations for the day.

KORE

OVERVIEW: This lifestyle and gift boutique features a wide selection of well-designed goods.

COST: $$

ADDRESS: 1200 Villa Pl

NEIGHBORHOOD: Edgehill Village

HOURS: Mon – Sat, 10am – 5pm
Sun, noon – 5pm

PHONE: 1.615.516.4110

WEBSITE: korenashville.com

INSTAGRAM: @korenashville

ATMOSPHERE: Located in historic Edgehill Village, Kore features high ceilings and lots of gorgeous natural light.

HIGHLIGHTS: It's obvious the owner puts great thought into picking out each item for the store. Each piece is unique, well-designed, and of the highest quality. You'll find books, greeting cards, beauty products, clothing, and so much more.

INSIDER TIPS: It's the perfect place to find the perfect gift and they offer gift wrapping too. It's nestled among many other great shops and restaurants, so make a day out of it and check them all out!

PHOTOS (LEFT TO RIGHT):
Sarah Patton (@sarahcharlottepatton)
Mali Schneiter (@malikathleen)

WRITER:
Abby Reuther (@abby.reuther)

DRAPER JAMES

OVERVIEW: This is Reese Witherspoon's flagship store honoring all things Southern, from women's clothing to accessories to home decor.

COST: $$

ADDRESS: 2608 12th Ave S

NEIGHBORHOOD: 12 South

HOURS: Mon – Wed, 10am – 6pm
Thu – Sat, 10am – 7pm
Sun, 11am – 5pm

PHONE: 1.615.997.3601

WEBSITE: draperjames.com

INSTAGRAM: @draperjames

ATMOSPHERE: The blue and white striped wall is becoming iconic. Inside, Draper James is clean, stylish, modern, and homey.

HIGHLIGHTS: The featured style has been coined "affordable luxury" and is designed to capture the grace and charm of the South while speaking to modern women. From product names to t-shirts with cute Southern sayings, each element pays tribute to the Southern lifestyle.

INSIDER TIPS: Everyone knows Southerners and football go together like biscuits and gravy. Draper James features a tailgate-inspired line to get you outfitted for game day.

PHOTOS (LEFT TO RIGHT):
Victoria Harman (@HauteontheSpot1)
and Liz Rogers (@lizrogersxoxo)

WRITER: Kristen Shoates (@kristennicole86)

ABEDNEGO

OVERVIEW: This small boutique specializes in women and men's clothing, accessories, and home goods.

COST: $$

ADDRESS: 1210 4th Ave N

NEIGHBORHOOD: Germantown

HOURS: Tues – Sat, 11am – 6pm
Sun, noon – 5pm

PHONE: 1.615.712.6028

WEBSITE: abednegoboutique.com

INSTAGRAM: @abednegonash

ATMOSPHERE: The shop is very clean, crisp, and white with everything well organized and on gorgeous display. A vibrant energy fills the boutique, and you'll get a warm, genuine greeting from the staff. I have always been provided with excellent assistance and guidance with decision making when needed.

HIGHLIGHTS: The owner fills her store with classic yet unique pieces. Items at ABEDNEGO are reasonably priced, and I have a hard time not buying everything in the store.

INSIDER TIPS: This is my go-to place when I'm in need of a gift. Something can always be found—candles, purses, necklaces, shirts, and much more.

PHOTOS (LEFT TO RIGHT):
Sara Estensen (@saraestensen) and Mali Schneiter (@malikathleen)

WRITER: Holly Darnell (@hollywood_25)

HAYMAKERS & COMPANY

OVERVIEW: You'll find upscale men's clothing, a full-service barber, and made-to-measure clothing.

COST: $$$

ADDRESS: 3307 West End Ave

NEIGHBORHOOD: West End

HOURS: Mon, noon – 6pm
Tues – Sat, 10am – 6pm

PHONE: 1.615.810.9442

WEBSITE: haymakersandco.com

INSTAGRAM: @haymakersnashville

ATMOSPHERE: You'll feel at home when you walk in, not just because of the rich, manly decor, but because their customer service is top-notch. Whether you're there for a hair cut, custom fitting, or shopping for your man (like me), they make it the best and easiest process.

HIGHLIGHTS: Need a drink to help you shop? Good thing drinks are on the house!

They carefully select well-made products from brands with a purpose, so you know your dime is going toward the very best.

INSIDER TIPS: Men, I know you don't like to shop, but believe me when I say you'll love your experience at Haymakers.

PHOTOS (LEFT TO RIGHT):
Abby Reuther (@abby.reuther) and
GROWN Magazine (@grownmag)

WRITER: Abby Reuther (@abby.reuther)

BATCH NASHVILLE

OVERVIEW: Batch is home to locally made gifts and food straight from Nashville makers and artisans.

COST: $

ADDRESS: 900 Rosa L Parks Blvd (inside the Nashville Farmers' Market)

NEIGHBORHOOD: Downtown

HOURS: Every day, 10am – 4pm

PHONE: 1.615.913.3912

WEBSITE: batchusa.com

INSTAGRAM: @batchusa

ATMOSPHERE: Located in the center of Germantown's Farmers Market, Batch is the perfect spot for last-minute pick-me-up gifts. Complete with unfinished wood and stamped signage, the spot has the feel of a weekend pop-up shop with tons of local goods for the new homeowner, new mom, or new Nashvillian.

HIGHLIGHTS: Everything is local and handmade, perfect for gifts with an added personal, Southern touch. They also offer Gift Batches (similar to a gift basket) if you're unsure of what to pick up for a wedding, corporate event, or housewarming party.

INSIDER TIPS: All goods are available online too! So if you pick up something you want more of, just look 'em up!

PHOTOS (LEFT TO RIGHT):
Kristin Walker (@walkerfeedco)
Sarah Patton (@sarahcharlottepatton)

WRITER: Aubrey Hine (@aubreyhine)

TWO OLD HIPPIES

OVERVIEW: This is an eclectic, one-stop shop for all your fashion and gifting needs.

COST: $$$

ADDRESS: 401 12th Ave S

NEIGHBORHOOD: The Gulch

HOURS: Mon – Thur, 10am – 7pm
Fri – Sat, 10am – 8pm
Sun, 11am – 6pm

PHONE: 1.615.254.7999

WEBSITE: twooldhippies.com

INSTAGRAM: @twooldhippies

ATMOSPHERE: A bohemian dream shop and a Nashville staple, this large store has hip and unique apparel you won't find in any other local stores.

HIGHLIGHTS: You can spend hours finding all the treasures you never knew you needed. This is the place where you can find something for everyone on your list while you pick up a few things for yourself. You may also catch a live show.

INSIDER TIPS: The shoe section and the baby/kid section are my personal favorites. You can make your nieces and nephews future rock stars. They also have amazing sales a few times a year that you DO NOT want to miss.

PHOTOS (LEFT TO RIGHT):
Stephanie Torre (@stephtorre) and Abby Reuther (@abby.reuther)

WRITER: Allison Holley (@appleandoaknash)

MODA BOUTIQUE

OVERVIEW: *Moda,* meaning "fashion" in Italian, says it all—it's a edgy, trendy women's boutique.

COST: $$$

ADDRESS: 2511 12th Ave S

NEIGHBORHOOD: 12 South

HOURS: Sun – Mon, noon – 5pm
Tues – Sat, 10:30am – 6pm

PHONE: 1.615.298.2271

WEBSITE: modanashville.com

INSTAGRAM: @modanashville

ATMOSPHERE: Located in a cute little old house, the shop is welcoming and cozy.

HIGHLIGHTS: There's a mix of styles, making it easy for anyone to find that perfect piece that meets their style. Along with a mix of styles, they also have a great mix of dressy and casual—find the perfect cocktail dress or Sunday casual low-key outfit.

They get new arrivals DAILY, so you can basically go there every day and treat yourself!

INSIDER TIPS: It's among many other great shops and restaurants on 12 South, so make a day of shopping and eating. Sounds like the perfect Saturday to me.

PHOTOS (LEFT TO RIGHT):
Aubrey Hine (@aubreyhine)
Meagan Rose (@themeaganrose)

WRITER: Abby Reuther (@abby.reuther)

NATIVE + NOMAD

OVERVIEW: This women's boutique has a wide range of fashion pieces and price points. There's a mix of pieces from local designers, well-established designers, and up-and-coming designers.

COST: $$

ADDRESS: 1813 21st Ave S

NEIGHBORHOOD: Hillsboro Village

HOURS: Mon – Wed, 10am – 6pm
Thur – Sat, 10am – 7pm
Sun, noon – 5pm

PHONE: 1.615.840.7409

WEBSITE: shopnativeandnomad.com

INSTAGRAM: @shopnativeandnomad

ATMOSPHERE: In the heart of the popular Hillsboro neighborhood, it's surrounded by other shops and restaurants. It's a hip little shop with all the Nashville vibes.

HIGHLIGHTS: They carefully select each of their items to make sure they've been ethically produced. You can always feel good about wearing their clothes.

They carry the perfect mix of on-trend items and your everyday staples.

INSIDER TIPS: There's an awesome sale rack in the back—hit it up.

PHOTOS (LEFT TO RIGHT):
Tanya Rustigian (@trustjewelry)
Holly Darnell (@hollywood_25)

WRITER: Abby Reuther (@abby.reuther)

CASTILLEJA

OVERVIEW: A castilleja, also known as the Indian paintbrush, is an adorable flower that grows out west. That pretty much describes this little lifestyle shop. It's locally owned and operated and dusted with personality, music, and stuff that you'll love.

COST: $$

ADDRESS: 1200 Villa Pl #403

NEIGHBORHOOD: Edgehill Village

HOURS: Mon – Sat, 10am – 6pm
Sun, noon – 4pm

PHONE: 1.615.730.5367

WEBSITE: castillejanashville.com

INSTAGRAM: @castillejanashville

ATMOSPHERE: The small interior is jam-packed with colorful gifts full of color and personality.

HIGHLIGHTS: You'll find unique one-of-a-kind gifts and clothes. There's always new goodies filling the shelves.

INSIDER TIPS: The mark-down shelf is hidden. And I'm not telling you where it is. (It's hidden by the baby stuff in the corner. Note: WHY don't they make some of this baby stuff in my size?!) Also, DO NOT, I repeat: DO NOT go to Castilleja after having a few Kentucky Mules at Burger Up…

PHOTOS (LEFT TO RIGHT):
Rosemary R. (@GardenKeyCo)
Kelly Christine Sutton (@kellychristinesutton)

WRITER: Kate Moore (@moore_kate)

BLOOM FLOWERS

OVERVIEW: Bloom is more than just a flower shop. It's a hidden gem tucked off of Belmont Boulevard. Bloom not only caters to your floral needs, but they also have gifts for every occasion.

COST: $

ADDRESS: 1517 Dallas Ave

NEIGHBORHOOD: Belmont Blvd

HOURS: Mon – Fri, 9am – 6pm
Sat, 10am – 5pm

PHONE: 1.615.385.2402

WEBSITE: nashvillebloom.com

INSTAGRAM: @nashvillebloom

ATMOSPHERE: The store is packed with gifts for men and women. No need to run to the mall or fight for parking when there's a local store with affordable presents. Bloom has thought of everything—you'll seriously swoon over the baby selection, and there's a plethora of local goodies, candles galore, and an entire card wall to choose from.

HIGHLIGHTS: It's the perfect place to pop in and grab that one-of-a-kind thoughtful gift. If you're like me, you'll leave with a present for a friend and a treat for yourself!

INSIDER TIPS: Their flower cooler is stocked with pre-made arrangements as well as single stems.

PHOTOS: Abby Reuther (@abby.reuther)

WRITER: Sarah Patton (@sarahcharlottepatton)

PIECES BOUTIQUE

OVERVIEW: Pieces is an affordable small boutique with an eclectic collection of women's clothing and accessories.

COST: $$

ADDRESS: 500 Madison St

NEIGHBORHOOD: Germantown

HOURS: Tues, noon – 6pm
Wed – Fri, 11am – 7pm
Sat, 11am – 5pm
Sun, 11am – 4pm

PHONE: 1.615.678.8271

WEBSITE: piecesfashion.com

INSTAGRAM: @piecesfashion

ATMOSPHERE: It's packed with clothing and accessories! They definitely put every inch of that store to good use.

HIGHLIGHTS: They carry a variety of styles, which means you'll probably find something new for your closet every single time. They carry a large selection of Project 615 t-shirts, which make for great Nashville souvenirs and gifts. For convenience, they have a great online shop.

INSIDER TIPS: It's street parking only and the few spots on the street out front are usually taken. Park on 5th and grab a coffee from Red Bicycle to sip on while you shop.

PHOTOS (LEFT TO RIGHT):
Aubrey Hine (@aubreyhine)
Holly Darnell (@hollywood_25)

WRITER: Abby Reuther (@abby.reuther)

CONSIDER THE WLDFLWRS

OVERVIEW: This is a whimsical jewelry shop where every piece is handcrafted with care.

COST: $$$

ADDRESS: 1807 9th Ave North

NEIGHBORHOOD: Buchannan Arts District

HOURS: Mon – Fri, 11am – 6pm
Sat, 11am – 5pm

PHONE: 1.629.888.9328

WEBSITE: considerthewldflwrs.com

INSTAGRAM: @considerthewldflwrs

ATMOSPHERE: Sun-kissed walls and soft lighting reveal stunning details of each necklace, ring, bracelet and earring set. A large antique rug and aromatic candles tie the quaint shop together, giving you that one-of-a-kind, handmade feel.

HIGHLIGHTS: The boutique's delicate, hand-crafted pieces allow you to layer and enhance your current style. The simple pieces can be paired with jewelry you currently own, adding a glimpse of Nashville into your everyday lifestyle. Home products are also available and make wonderful gifts!

INSIDER TIPS: They also design and sell engagement and wedding rings for both women and men. Follow their bridal line at @considerbridal.

PHOTOS:
Consider the Wldflwrs (@considerthewldflwrs)

WRITER: Aubrey Hine (@aubreyhine)

THE MILL BOUTIQUE

OVERVIEW: This women's clothing and accessory boutique features goods at an affordable price.

COST: $$

ADDRESS: 812 51st Ave N

NEIGHBORHOOD: The Nations

HOURS: Tues – Sat, 11am – 6pm
Sun, noon – 4pm

PHONE: 1.615.873.4432

WEBSITE: millnashville.com

INSTAGRAM: @shopthemill

ATMOSPHERE: It's bright and colorful, with lots to look at and try on. The ladies are there to help you find the perfect outfit and accessories too; they have a great selection.

HIGHLIGHTS: They have a wide variety of clothing items, but they also have jewelry, shoes, purses, sunglasses, and gift items like cards, notebooks, candles, decorated wine glasses, and so much more.

INSIDER TIPS: They started their business by selling clothing on Instagram, so it's safe to say they have a great Instagram feed that keeps you up-to-date on the latest styles and arrivals.

PHOTOS: Lauren Miller (The Mill Boutique) (@shopthemill)

WRITER: Abby Reuther (@abby.reuther)

PROJECT 615

OVERVIEW: This philanthropic t-shirt and apparel company benefits the local community of Nashville. The majority of their t-shirts are Nashville-themed, making them great gifts and souvenirs for all those Nashville lovers.

COST: $$

ADDRESS: 1006 Fatherland St #205
For their other location, please visit the website.

NEIGHBORHOOD: East Nashville

HOURS: Sun – Thur, 12 – 6pm
Fri – Sat, 11am – 6pm

PHONE: 1.615.835.3588

WEBSITE: project615.org

INSTAGRAM: @project615

ATMOSPHERE: It's located at the Shoppes on Fatherland among other local shops, restaurants, and other small businesses. The shop is small and the walls are lined with colorful t-shirts.

HIGHLIGHTS: They have an online shop for those who can't make it to their Fatherland shop.

INSIDER TIPS: Lots of local shops carry their apparel too. Visit their website and follow them on Instagram to keep up-to-date on their pop-up shops at local festivals and events.

PHOTOS (LEFT TO RIGHT):
Brooke Rosolino (@Cravewellnow)
Olivia Laskowski (@o.ray)

WRITER: Abby Reuther (@abby.reuther)

FLWR SHOP

OVERVIEW: They will make all your flower and plant dreams come true.

COST: $$

ADDRESS: 123 S 11th St

NEIGHBORHOOD: East Nashville

HOURS: Mon – Fri, 9am – 7pm
Sat, 10am – 4pm

PHONE: 1.615.401.9124

WEBSITE: flwrshop.com

INSTAGRAM: @flwrshop

ATMOSPHERE: Located in a dreamy historic home, where the romantic staircase, dramatic floral wallpaper, and gorgeous velvet couch are enough to make you swoon. It's packed full of giant plants, stunning flowers, and potted succulents. The owners are lovely, welcoming, and full of all plant and floral knowledge.

HIGHLIGHTS: While they do have gorgeous flowers, this isn't just a flower shop. The plants are the show stealer. If you are a plant killer, have no fear. The staff will share their wealth of knowledge with you and help you pick out and care for the perfect plant for you.

INSIDER TIPS: They offer delivery and have a flower of the month club.

PHOTOS (LEFT TO RIGHT):
Jessie Schultz (@callmeschultz)
Steffi Yoon (@steffi.yoon)

WRITER: Allison Holley (@appleandoaknash)

GRIMEY'S NEW & PRELOVED MUSIC

OVERVIEW: Grimey's is a treasure trove for the music-loving bargain hunter.

COST: $

ADDRESS: 1604 8th Ave S

NEIGHBORHOOD: 8th Ave

HOURS: Mon – Fri, 11am – 8pm
Sat, 10am – 8pm
Sun, 1 – 6pm

PHONE: 1.615.254.4801

WEBSITE: grimeys.com

INSTAGRAM: @grimeys

ATMOSPHERE: The storefront is more of a house you'd normally see near a university, with enough room in the backyard for big parties and intimate concerts. You don't have to be well-versed in music to appreciate the love, respect, and history of each vinyl album and CD inside the snug walls of Grimey's.

HIGHLIGHTS: You could go rummaging through the enormous collections on any given day and find Brian Wilson, Stevie Nicks, Elvis, and the like, then turn around to see Sturgill Simpson, Leon Bridges, Grimes, and Alabama Shakes in the same breath.

INSIDER TIPS: Check their website for in-store shows and other happenings!

PHOTOS (LEFT TO RIGHT):
Rachel Anderson (@rachelmarieanderson) and Jessica Steddom (@jessicasteddom, @projectmusicEC and @entrecenter)

WRITER: Kelley Griggs (@kelleyboothe)

OAK NASHVILLE

OVERVIEW: This home decor store has the perfect amount of rustic Southern charm and design. The store's acronym, meaning "one of a kind," perfectly describes the types of items you'll discover there.

COST: $$

ADDRESS: 4200 Charlotte Ave

NEIGHBORHOOD: Sylvan Park

HOURS: Tues – Sat, 10am – 5pm
Sun, noon – 4pm

PHONE: 1.615.477.6338

WEBSITE: oaknashville.com

INSTAGRAM: @oaknashville

ATMOSPHERE: It's a good-size store; not too large, not too small. It's calm, relaxing, and inviting.

HIGHLIGHTS: It's truly a place to find one-of-a-kind pieces for your home. It also has lots of great options for small gifts. They support local by carrying local artisans' and small businesses' goodies.

INSIDER TIPS: Go there to decorate your whole house—really. I discovered this gem right after I finished decorating my new house and boy was I bummed. I might need to redecorate soon, very soon.

PHOTOS (LEFT TO RIGHT):
Mali Schneiter (@malikathleen) and
Sarah Patton (@sarahcharlottepatton)

WRITER:
Abby Reuther (@abby.reuther)

HATCH SHOW PRINT

OVERVIEW: Since 1879, Hatch Show Print has been creating iconic and memorable designs with classic letterpress printing.

COST: $$

ADDRESS: 224 5th Ave S

NEIGHBORHOOD: Sobro

HOURS: Sun – Wed, 9:30am – 6pm
Thur – Sat, 9:30am – 8pm

PHONE: 1.615.577.7710

WEBSITE: hatchshowprint.com

INSTAGRAM: @hatchshowprint

ATMOSPHERE: Originally housed on Lower Broadway, Hatch Show Print moved to 5th Avenue (inside the Country Music Hall of Fame and Museum) in 2014, where it continues to uphold the tradition of old-style letterpress poster printing and thrive under the mission William Hatch instilled in the company when it began operation in 1879.

HIGHLIGHTS: Tours of the famous letterpress shop are available for booking. The experience allows guests to operate some of the tools and learn the letterpress process the way it has been done for centuries.

INSIDER TIPS: They take custom poster and design orders.

PHOTOS (LEFT TO RIGHT):
Haley Turnbull (@haleyturnbull) and Farhan Rehmani (@netpunk76)

WRITER: Kelley Griggs (@kelleyboothe)

WHISKEY WATER

OVERVIEW: A women's boutique that is perfectly described by them as "clothes for the rock & roll loving, whiskey drinking rebel in all of us." You'll find one-of-a-kind clothing pieces, whiskey-themed t-shirts, and statement accessories.

COST: $$

ADDRESS: 1006 Fatherland St #103

NEIGHBORHOOD: East Nashville

HOURS: Tues – Sat, 11am – 5pm
Sun, noon – 4pm

WEBSITE: shopwhiskeywater.com

INSTAGRAM: @whiskeywaternashville

ATMOSPHERE: Nestled in the Shoppes on Fatherland, this small shop is one you don't want to miss. Its small interior is filled with tons of sassy options for your next perfect outfit.

HIGHLIGHTS: The store and clothing line is run by founder and editor of the popular style blog The Whiskey Wolf. If you haven't checked out her blog, you're missing out.

INSIDER TIPS: Follow them on Instagram; they do a great job keeping their followers up-to-date with new arrivals and how to put together the perfect outfit.

PHOTOS (LEFT TO RIGHT):
Abby Reuther (@abby.reuther)
Aubrey Hine (@aubreyhine)

WRITER:
Abby Reuther (@abby.reuther)

PARNASSUS BOOKS

OVERVIEW: This independent local bookstore has shelves full of books from floor to ceiling.

COST: $

ADDRESS: 3900 Hillsboro Pike, Suite 14

NEIGHBORHOOD: Green Hills

HOURS: Mon – Sat, 10am – 8pm
Sun, noon – 5pm

PHONE: 1.615.953.2243

WEBSITE: parnassusbooks.net

INSTAGRAM: @parnassusbooks

ATMOSPHERE: It's everything you'd want the perfect bookstore to be: walls and tables filled with books, that book smell, shop dogs wandering, and cozy spaces to read.

HIGHLIGHTS: SHOP DOGS! I repeat, DOGS! What's better than being greeted by dogs as you find your perfect next book to read?

You can also find their mobile book van cruising around town or at local events and festivals.

INSIDER TIPS: They have events almost every day, so check their online events calendar. Whether you want to get involved in a book club, meet an author, or attend a book reading, they have an option for everyone who loves books and stories!

PHOTOS: Parnassus Books (@parnassusbooks)

WRITER: Abby Reuther (@abby.reuther)

VINNIE LOUISE

OVERVIEW: Vinnie Louise is a women's clothing and accessory shop. Their tag line says it all: "Stylishly selected clothes, affordably edited prices."

COST: $$

ADDRESS: 521 Gallatin Ave
For their other locations, please visit the website.

NEIGHBORHOOD: East Nashville

HOURS: Tues – Fri, 11am – 6pm
Sat, noon – 4pm

WEBSITE: vinnielouise.com
Instagram: @vinnielouise

ATMOSPHERE: Located in the Shops at Porter East, the store is light and refreshing and the ladies who work there are great at helping you find the perfect outfit or accessory.

HIGHLIGHTS: They have tops, pants, dresses, ponchos, cardigans, purses, shoes, jewelry, and fun gift items like candles and cards.

They have a great online shop that they are constantly updating with new arrivals.

INSIDER TIPS: Their Instagram is a great way to keep up-to-date with their new arrivals.

They also have a men's clothing store, Jack Randall. Ladies, treat your man.

PHOTOS (LEFT TO RIGHT):
Claudia Cofer (@Claudiakayphoto)
Cody Stallings (@Codystallingsphotography)

WRITER:
Abby Reuther (@abby.reuther)

HER BOOKSHOP

OVERVIEW: This independent bookstore has the perfect tag line: "A nook for people who love beautiful books."

COST: $$

ADDRESS: 1043 W Eastland Ave

NEIGHBORHOOD: East Nashville

HOURS: Mon – Fri, 11am – 6pm
Sat, 10am – 6pm
Sun, 11am – 4pm

WEBSITE: herbookshop.com

INSTAGRAM: @her_bookshop

ATMOSPHERE: Her Bookshop has moved locations, and boy is their new location nice! It's much larger than the last location which means . . . MORE BOOKS! It still has the same inviting atmosphere, just as you'd imagine a perfect bookstore to be.

HIGHLIGHTS: Joelle, the owner, is a 20-year publishing veteran and author to more than 15 books, so you can guarantee each book was carefully selected. She aims to surprise people with books that they've never heard of. There's a wide range of topics and at all price points, which makes it the perfect bookstore for everyone.

INSIDER TIPS: You are able to place special orders for books and can pick them up at the store within about a week.

PHOTOS (LEFT TO RIGHT):
Abby Reuther (@abby.reuther)
Sarah Patton (@sarahcharlottepatton)

WRITER:
Abby Reuther (@abby.reuther)

ADVENTURE + ENTERTAINMENT

music venues

THE LISTENING ROOM CAFE

OVERVIEW: This is a music venue showcasing singers and songwriters, plus a great bar and Southern-inspired menu.

COST: $$

ADDRESS: 618 4th Ave S

NEIGHBORHOOD: Sobro

HOURS:
Mon – Fri, 11am – 3pm and 4pm – 11pm
Sat, 4pm – 11pm

PHONE: 1.615.259.3600

WEBSITE: listeningroomcafe.com

INSTAGRAM: @listeningroomcafe

ATMOSPHERE: There's an atmosphere where artists can be heard and fans can truly enjoy the listening experience. The brick, loft-style interior, soft lighting, and patio make for a gorgeous setting while honoring Music City's unique talent.

HIGHLIGHTS: There are up-and-coming songwriters and artists as well as big names in music. It is one of the best places to get a taste of the songwriting scene and to hear your favorite songs from writers themselves.

INSIDER TIPS: Consider making a reservation for dinner or brunch. There's complimentary valet parking with the purchase of dinner.

PHOTOS: Listening Room Cafe (@listeningroomcafe)

WRITER: Kristen Shoates (@kristennicole86)

THE BASEMENT

OVERVIEW: This is the perfect place if you're looking for some local artists. The venue isn't going to impress you with its aesthetics, but the real and raw talent will blow your mind.

COST: $

ADDRESS: 1604 8th Ave S
For their other location, please visit the website.

NEIGHBORHOOD: 8th Ave

HOURS: *Depends on shows. Please visit their website for the schedule.*

PHONE: 1.615.645-9174

WEBSITE: thebasementnashville.com

INSTAGRAM: @thebasementnash

ATMOSPHERE: It's a small, grungy basement located underneath Grimey's. It honestly couldn't be more perfect.

HIGHLIGHTS: They have New Faces Nite on Tuesday to introduce the community to up-and-coming artists. If you're ballin' on a budget, they have lots of FREE shows. Check their calendar to purchase tickets in advance.

INSIDER TIPS: Get there early if you want to snag an actual seat. Since the space isn't huge, you'll be left with standing room only.

PHOTOS (LEFT TO RIGHT):
Michael Reuther (@michaelreuther)
OurVinyl (@ourvinyl)

WRITER: Sarah Patton (@sarahcharlottepatton)

EXIT/IN

OVERVIEW: This quintessential Nashville music venue hosts a variety of local and national alternative acts nearly every night of the week.

COST: $$

ADDRESS: 2208 Elliston Pl

NEIGHBORHOOD: Elliston Place

HOURS: *Depends on shows. Please visit their website for the schedule.*

PHONE: 1.615.321.3340

WEBSITE: exitin.com

INSTAGRAM: @exit_in

ATMOSPHERE: It's a no-frills club with all the staples: expansive floor, stage, and bar. Created as a haven for artists and fans of genres other than Nashville's typical honky tonk scene, expect to hear rock, punk, soul, hip hop, and more.

HIGHLIGHTS: It has hosted an impressive list of artists, including Etta James, The Talking Heads, and countless others. These artists' names are memorialized on the walls—the classic monikers in white type on a black backdrop have become the club's most iconic feature.

INSIDER TIPS: There are no seats on the main floor, so wear comfortable shoes and be prepared to stand. The club is 18 and up unless otherwise noted.

PHOTOS (LEFT TO RIGHT):
Cover Nashville (@covernashville) and OurVinyl (@ourvinyl)

WRITER: Kristen Shoates (@kristennicole86)

THE BLUEBIRD CAFE

OVERVIEW: It's one of the world's most iconic music venues, recognized for songwriter's performances and for being the discovery place for some of the most talented musicians around.

COST: $$

ADDRESS: 4104 Hillsboro Pike

NEIGHBORHOOD: Green Hills

HOURS: Two shows every night:
Sun, 6pm and 8pm
Mon, 6pm and 9:30pm
Tues – Thur, 6pm and 9pm
Fri – Sat, 6:30pm and 9:30pm

PHONE: 1.615.383.1461

WEBSITE: bluebirdcafe.com

INSTAGRAM: @bluebirdcafetn

ATMOSPHERE: This 90-seat venue is located in a small strip mall. It has maintained its hole-in-the-wall style all these years and you really get that sense of Music City history.

HIGHLIGHTS: Most nights, three to four songwriters sit in the center of the room and take turns playing their songs. A little history—Garth Brooks was discovered there!

INSIDER TIPS: Get there early to get a spot in line. Keep that mouth zipped during the performances—the music is taken very seriously.

PHOTOS (LEFT TO RIGHT):
Michael Reuther (@michaelreuther)
Megan Davey (@ChasingDavies)

WRITER: Abby Reuther (@abby.reuther)

STATION INN

OVERVIEW: It's widely known as one of the best bluegrass venues around.

COST: $

ADDRESS: 402 12th Ave S

NEIGHBORHOOD: The Gulch

HOURS: Every day, doors at 7pm and shows start at 9pm

PHONE: 1.615.255.3307

WEBSITE: stationinn.com

ATMOSPHERE: A simple no-frills space makes it the perfect laid-back venue to focus solely on the bluegrass music. Even the food is simple—nachos, hot dogs, and pizza.

HIGHLIGHTS: Famous artists are known to be among the guests and even hop on stage for a song or two.

INSIDER TIPS: They do not take reservations or sell tickets ahead of time. It's a first-come first-served basis—be prepared to get there early and wait in line outside.

Cover fees are taken at the door and they only accept cash. Credit cards are accepted once inside for food and drinks.

Check the online calendar, even a few hours before show time, because their shows are subject to change at any time without notice.

PHOTOS (LEFT TO RIGHT):
OurVinyl (@ourvinyl)
Michael Reuther (@michaelreuther)

WRITER: Abby Reuther (@abby.reuther)

ADVENTURE + ENTERTAINMENT

parks

RADNOR LAKE STATE PARK

OVERVIEW: 1,200 acres of rolling hills, paved paths, and dirt trails make this park accessible for people of all ages and fitness levels.

COST: FREE

ADDRESS: 1160 Otter Creek Rd

NEIGHBORHOOD: Near Green Hills

HOURS: Every day, 6am – dark

PHONE: 1.615.373.3467

WEBSITE: radnorlake.org

INSTAGRAM: @radnorlake

ATMOSPHERE: I'm amazed how you can simply be a few miles from downtown, yet you're encompassed by the complete stillness of nature at Radnor.

HIGHLIGHTS: Wildlife roams freely—you'll see white-tailed deer, river otters, turkeys, eagles, and turtles.

INSIDER TIPS: Want to volunteer and help keep this park beautiful? Meet at the visitor center off Granny White Pike on the fourth Saturday of each month from 8am to noon to assist with the upkeep of Radnor.

PHOTOS (LEFT TO RIGHT):
Gai Phanalasy (@gaichicken)
Virginia White (@virgy_white)

WRITER:
Sarah Patton (@sarahcharlottepatton)

CENTENNIAL PARK

OVERVIEW:
Right off West End Avenue—one of Nashville's main thoroughfares, lined with restaurants, hotels and condos—Centennial Park is a true city park, an expansive green space that offers running paths, live events and festivals, and space to play against the backdrop of Nashville's skyline.

COST: FREE

ADDRESS: 2500 West End Ave

NEIGHBORHOOD: West End

HOURS: Every day, dawn - 11pm

COMMUNITY FAVORITE:
The Parthenon, an iconic, even if borrowed, landmark in Nashville, also serves as a city art museum with permanent galleries and rotating exhibits. It is open Tuesday to Sunday from 9am to 4:30pm and Sunday from 12:30 to 4:30pm. Even Mick Jagger recently made a visit to The Parthenon the last time the Stones were in town.

PHOTOS (LEFT TO RIGHT):
Lindsay Bennett (@lindsaynicholedesigns)
Aubrey Hine (@aubreyhine)
Dorothy Wallis (@peachthedoodle)
Abby Reuther (@abby.reuther)

WRITER:
Kristen Shoates (@kristennicole86)

ATMOSPHERE:

Family-friendly with a playground, pond for feeding the ducks, and relatively easy walking paths, Centennial Park is a multi-cultural gathering spot in the heart of the city. Beautiful landscaping, plenty of green space, trails for exercise, and proximity to restaurants and businesses makes Centennial Park a popular spot for locals and tourists alike.

HIGHLIGHTS:

At the center of the park is The Parthenon, a life-size replica of the Grecian landmark and an icon left over from the 1897 Tennessee Centennial and International Exposition. An expansive lawn extends from the structure, offering a popular place for sunbathing, Frisbee, and flag football, while a one-mile paved trail through the heart of the park draws runners, walkers, and cyclists.

INSIDER TIPS:

Centennial Park hosts events nearly every weekend, from international craft festivals to Shakespeare to swing dancing to the popular Musician's Corner, a free showcase of local musicians each Saturday in the spring and fall. Check the calendar before you go: you might want to plan around one that catches your fancy; or, if you're looking for a more relaxing experience, try to catch an off weekend. The park is also a popular perch for some of Nashville's favorite food trucks, so be sure to bring some cash to sample the local cuisine.

PERCY WARNER PARK

OVERVIEW: A city escape with multiple dirt trails, paved roads, and horse trails, Percy Warner Park even has a great golf course.

COST: FREE

ADDRESS: 7311 US Hwy 100

NEIGHBORHOOD: Belle Meade

HOURS: Every day, dawn - 11pm

WEBSITE: warnerparks.org

INSTAGRAM: @warnerparknaturecenter

ATMOSPHERE: Rolling hills and beautiful nature make you feel like you're miles from the city. Sometimes you won't see a single person; sometimes you'll see a bunch.

HIGHLIGHTS: The stairs at the Belle Meade Boulevard entrance are a BEAST—and I say that in the best way possible. You'll get to the top and look back thinking you just climbed a mountain.

INSIDER TIPS: Don't go when I go because then it will get busy! Also, don't go after it rains. #mudeverywere #mydoglikestolieinit

Nashville does an incredible job at taking care of our park system. It's our job to love them and take good care of them. Please continue to care for them by parking in designated areas and respecting the horse riding only signs.

PHOTOS (LEFT TO RIGHT):
Bonnie Willoughby (@bonlove) and Tori Perry (@tori_has)

WRITER: Kate Moore (@moore_kate)

entertainment

ZANIES COMEDY NIGHT CLUB

OVERVIEW: Zanies has been Nashville's popular comedy club for over 30 years. Local acts and famous comedians take the stage and make the crowd squeal with laughter.

COST: $$

ADDRESS: 2025 8th Ave S

NEIGHBORHOOD: 8th Ave

HOURS: Mon – Tues, 10am – 6pm
Wed – Thur, 10am – 9pm
Fri, 9am – 11pm
Sat, noon – 2am
Sun, 2 – 9pm

PHONE: 1.615.269.0221

WEBSITE: nashville.zanies.com

INSTAGRAM: @zaniesnashville

ATMOSPHERE: There's a main floor and balcony seating. Smiles and laughter fill the room, making for a happy and positive atmosphere.

HIGHLIGHTS: There's a good food and drink menu. Note that there is a two item minimum required for each person inside the club.

INSIDER TIPS: Seating is first-come first-served, so if you have a large group and want to sit together get there EARLY (at least an hour) and wait in line outside.

PHOTOS (LEFT TO RIGHT):
Abby Reuther (@abby.reuther)
Mommy Tonk - Stacie Burrows and Shannon Noel (@mommytonk)

WRITER: Abby Reuther (@abby.reuther)

NASHVILLE PEDAL TAVERN

OVERVIEW: It wasn't voted the #1 Outdoor Activity in Nashville for no reason. Hop on these 15-passenger bicycles for 2 hours, take in the Nashville sites, and enjoy a cold brew or two (or five: we won't judge).

COST: $$

ADDRESS: 1514A Demonbreun St

NEIGHBORHOOD: Demonbreun Hill

HOURS: Every day, 9:30am – 9:15pm Reservations required.

PHONE: 1.615.390.5038

WEBSITE: nashvillepedaltavern.com

INSTAGRAM: @nashvillepedaltavern

ATMOSPHERE: There are multiple routes so you can choose your scenery.

HIGHLIGHTS: Over the course of a 2-hour ride you'll stop at two to three bars where you can use your wristband for Nashville Pedal Tavern exclusive discounts.

INSIDER TIPS: Make reservations way in advance, like a month or two.

It's BYOB but they'll provide the cooler, ice, and cups.

PHOTOS (LEFT TO RIGHT):
Teresa, S (@teresamariaaa)
Holly Darnell (@hollywood_25)

WRITER: Abby Reuther (@abby.reuther)

THE ESCAPE GAME

OVERVIEW:
If you love a challenge and bragging rights are your cup of tea, The Escape Game is right up your alley and an F-U-N activity! Try to escape in under 60 minutes using clues, puzzles, and lots of brainpower. Try all of the rooms, and also bring your smartest friends, unless you like to lose.

COST: $$

ADDRESS: 162 3rd Ave N
For their other locations, please visit the website.

NEIGHBORHOOD: Downtown

HOURS: *Hours vary—please visit their website.*

PHONE: 1.615.647.8229

WEBSITE: NashvilleEscapeGame.com

INSTAGRAM: @TheEscapeGameNashville

COMMUNITY FAVORITE:
The Nashville room (obviously) is great, and escaping from the most challenging—Prison Break (it's a beast)—will give you bragging rights.

PHOTOS (LEFT TO RIGHT):
Aubrey Williams (@alwaysaubreyblog)
The Escape Game Nashville (@TheEscapeGameNashville)
Megan Vignola (@meganvignola)
Taylar Proctor (@teproctor)

WRITER:
Sarah Patton (@sarahcharlottepatton)

ATMOSPHERE:

I don't want to give you too many details because the surprise of each room is half the fun!

Your heart will be racing and your adrenaline will be pumping as you watch the staff close the door behind you. Make yourself useful and try to get out of the room before the countdown clock strikes 0:00. The time will fly by, and you'll be scrambling until the door opens—or your ego is bruised.

HIGHLIGHTS:

With multiple rooms to conquer, test your determination and IQ levels. Start easy or go straight for the hardest room. Either way, you'll definitely be coming back for more. It's the perfect spot for team-building activities, a challenge for your closest friends, or a date night activity for just the two of you.

INSIDER TIPS:

If you don't have enough people to make up an entire team, you can still play! Come by yourself or grab those who are available and make friends with people you don't know!

If you fail, don't let that discourage you—it's part of the fun and it just means you'll have to give it a second try. If you escape the first time, take on the challenge of another room—there are plenty to escape from.

OPRYLAND

OVERVIEW: A resort and convention center unlike any other, Opryland offers an indoor garden, restaurants, a European-inspired spa, pools, shopping, entertainment, and recreational activities.

COST: $$$

ADDRESS: 2800 Opryland Dr

NEIGHBORHOOD: Donelson

HOURS: Every day, 24 hours

PHONE: 1.615.889.1000

WEBSITE: gaylordopryland.com

ATMOSPHERE: One word: magical. There are nine acres of lush indoor botanical gardens with cascading waterfalls and a river under a glass atrium.

HIGHLIGHTS: Relax at their 27,000-foot European-inspired spa. Choose between their many restaurants—17 to be exact!

INSIDER TIPS: Visit during the holiday season. Their Christmas light display is pure magic with more than 2 million lights and festive holiday decor—plus, ice skating!

The Grand Ole Opry is only a 14-minute walk from the resort, so make sure to check out a show.

PHOTOS (LEFT TO RIGHT):
Elisa Gorman (@elisagorman)
Mari Rodriguez

WRITER: Abby Reuther (@abby.reuther)

HEALTH + BEAUTY

fitness

YOGA HARMONY

OVERVIEW: This yoga studio uses infrared heat and offers hot yoga, vinyasa flow, and restorative yoga.

COST: $$

ADDRESS: 4920 Charlotte Pike

NEIGHBORHOOD: The Nations

HOURS: *For the class schedule, please visit their website.*

PHONE: 1.615.823.3919

WEBSITE: yogaharmonynashville.com

INSTAGRAM: @yogaharmonynashville

ATMOSPHERE: You'll find a calm and relaxing atmosphere with dim mood lighting.

HIGHLIGHTS: Whether it's your first class or you are a seasoned yogi, the studio feels welcoming and the experienced teachers provide detailed instructions and offer corrective postures and repositioning throughout the class. Depending on what mood I'm in, I either do hot 60 or 75 or a flow class.

INSIDER TIPS: The new student special is $50 for 1 month unlimited, and a drop-in class is $18. A community class is available on Friday evenings, which allows for donations to be made to a chosen charity instead of the cost of a regular class.

PHOTOS (LEFT TO RIGHT):
Holly Darnell (@hollywood_25)
Mali Schneiter (@malikathleen)

WRITER: Holly Darnell (@hollywood_25)

NASHVILLE PADDLE COMPANY

OVERVIEW: Join a class for some FloYo, aka yoga on a paddle-board, take an intro to paddle boarding class, jump into a fitness on-board class, or rent a board for a few hours and enjoy the lake. You have lots of options!

COST: $$

ADDRESS: Percy Priest, Hamilton Creek Recreation Area, 2901 Bell Rd

HOURS: *Seasonal hours–please visit their website.*

PHONE: 1.615.682.1787

WEBSITE: nashvillepaddle.com

INSTAGRAM: @nashvillepaddle

ATMOSPHERE: You'll be surrounded by gorgeous Tennessee landscape on the water. It's relaxing, fun, challenging, outdoorsy, and empowering.

HIGHLIGHTS: GetFit615 and Shakti Power Yoga have classes on the paddle boards—check online for details!

INSIDER TIPS: NPC is offered on ClassPass. Take an intro class even if you've paddle boarded before. You can never learn too much!

PHOTOS (LEFT TO RIGHT):
Holly Myers (@_hollymyers_)
Nashville Paddle Company (@nashvillepaddle)

WRITER: Kate Moore (@moore_kate)

KRANK FIT

OVERVIEW: This cycle and strength fitness studio has a mission "to be the most efficient hour of your day."

COST: $$

ADDRESS: 2148 Bandywood Dr

NEIGHBORHOOD: Green Hills

HOURS: *For the class schedule, please visit their website below.*

PHONE: 1.615.549.0240

WEBSITE: krankfit.com

INSTAGRAM: @kranknash

ATMOSPHERE: The minute you step into Krank's cycling arena, you feel an intense wave of energy. The bikes are set close together in a crescent shape, with your trainer's bike highlighted in the center of the room. Once the lights go out, glowing floor lights illuminate and you're ready to sweat!

HIGHLIGHTS: Every instructor is unique in their own way. Check their website to view each individual's bio and playlist you think best fits your speed. Shoes and towels are available to use every class and showers are accessible to everyone.

INSIDER TIPS: Krank is available on ClassPass, so if you want to try cycling a few times before committing, this is the place! You might even spot a celebrity or two checking in.

PHOTOS: Aubrey Hine (@aubreyhine)

WRITER: Aubrey Hine (@aubreyhine)

GETFIT615

OVERVIEW:
This HIIT (high-intensity interval training) gym has classes lasting 45 minutes. The workout patterns vary weekly, with each day tailored to a specific theme (TRX Tuesday, Weighted Wednesdays, Total Body Thursday, Freedom Friday, and Mondays are a surprise). The workouts range from partner work to tabata to AMRAPS (as many rounds as possible), etc. The gym has a wide variety of equipment including rowers, kettle bells, bikes, ropes, boxes for box jumps, TRX suspensions, BOSUs, and medicine balls.

COST: $$

ADDRESS: 65 Music Square E

NEIGHBORHOOD: Music Row

HOURS: *For the class schedule, please visit their website.*

PHONE: 1.615.426.4785

WEBSITE: getfit615.com

INSTAGRAM: @getFIT615

COMMUNITY FAVORITE:
I love TRX Tuesdays because on that day, most exercises utilize the TRX, which is one of my favorite equipment pieces at the gym.

PHOTOS (LEFT TO RIGHT):
Sarah Mock (@sarahmock)
Shannon Frazier (@shannonbay)
Mary Roberts (@themurnburn)
Holly Darnell (@hollywood_25)

WRITER: Holly Darnell (@hollywood_25)

ATMOSPHERE:

It's housed in a basement with a bright green door, and the bright colors align with the gym's personality. The owner, Kate, is a bundle of energy who makes everyone feel welcome and encouraged at the gym. All of the class instructors have wonderful energy, motivation, and enthusiasm that are contagious throughout the workout. It's a positive environment where everyone feels like family. I've been going to the gym for 2 years, and I love that there is always variety to the workout.

HIGHLIGHTS:

Freedom Fridays: Each class chooses their exercises during the class period. People at the gym wear red, white, and blue or patriotic workout clothes, which makes for a fun end to the week.

Kate's black lab Emma is usually found at the gym, who also assists as an adorable motivator throughout the class.

INSIDER TIPS:

Try 30 days for $30 dollars, which is quite the steal! It's quite easy to get hooked after a month at the gym. Classes are also available on ClassPass. They partner with Shakti Yoga (a studio right above getFIT615) and you can pay $150 for unlimited yoga and gym classes.

They offer several activities each month outside of the gym, such as: Thursday Night Happy Hours, Hiking at the Fiery Gizzard, and climbing at Climb Nashville.

HOTBOX FITNESS

OVERVIEW: It's a one-of-a-kind kick-boxing class; a high-intensity group-fitness class where you'll punch and kick a 125-pound bag in a room set at 83 degrees.

COST: $$

ADDRESS: 125 12th Ave S

NEIGHBORHOOD: The Gulch

HOURS: *For the class schedule, please visit their website.*

PHONE: 1.615.881.5795

WEBSITE: hb4.me

INSTAGRAM: @hotboxnashville

ATMOSPHERE: If it's your first time, they bend over backward to make you feel comfortable. They'll wrap your hands, fit you for boxing gloves, and give you tips on how to dominate the class. Graffiti painted words and rap music blaring at all times will pump you up. The energy here gets you hyped!

HIGHLIGHTS: All levels of fitness are welcome. The instructors modify for the new people, but don't think they'll take it easy on you just because it's your first time.

INSIDER TIPS: Drink lots of water beforehand. Shoes aren't allowed on the mat so no need to wear your flashiest kicks. Bring a towel to wipe your face and hands.

PHOTOS (LEFT TO RIGHT):
Lindsay Alderson (@lindsayalderson)
Rachael Gabriel (@RachaelBruin)

WRITER: Sarah Patton (@sarahcharlottepatton)

CLIMB NASHVILLE

OVERVIEW: This climbing center is perfect for new climbers as well as experienced climbers. They have a great range of group fitness classes and yoga classes for their members too.

COST: $$

ADDRESS: 3600 Charlotte Ave
For their other location, please visit the website.

NEIGHBORHOOD: Sylvan Park

HOURS: Mon – Fri, 5am – 10 pm
Sat, 9am – 10pm
Sun, 12 – 10pm

PHONE: 1.615.463.7625

WEBSITE: climbnashville.com

INSTAGRAM: @climbnashville

ATMOSPHERE: Their staff is SUPER helpful and they're always glad to help you get outside of your comfort zone. It makes for a relaxed atmosphere. Even if it's your first time climbing and you're a little nervous, they'll put you at ease–you're in good hands!

HIGHLIGHTS: Climb is always full of people who are trying something new. The bouldering at Climb East and the speed wall at Climb West are amazing.

INSIDER TIPS: Go with a buddy and get in-house certified to belay each other.

PHOTOS (LEFT TO RIGHT):
Colby Lapolla (@colbylapolla) and Mali Schneiter (@malikathleen)

WRITER: Kate Moore (@moore_kate)

NASHVILLE B-CYCLE

OVERVIEW: It's a network of inexpensive bicycle rentals at 33 stations around Nashville.

COST: Starts at $5 for a 24-hour membership. *Fees and memberships on website.*

ADDRESS: *Station map on website.*

NEIGHBORHOOD: Throughout Nashville.

PHONE: 1.615.625.2153

WEBSITE: nashville.bcycle.com

INSTAGRAM: @nashvillebcycle

ATMOSPHERE: It's the great outdoors! Bike to work, run errands, hit up a greenway, or enjoy a ride with friends. Consider the exercise and fresh air as a bonus.

HIGHLIGHTS: The bikes have baskets to store your belongings, adjustable seats, lights, and different speed settings, making these easy for anyone to ride.

B-cycle partnered with the Mayor's Office and Nashville Metro Public Health Department to promote healthy and environmentally safe transportation in Nashville.

INSIDER TIPS: Annual and corporate memberships are available. If you're an annual member, your miles and calories burned are tracked in your B-cycle account.

PHOTOS (LEFT TO RIGHT):
Klaire Sawicki (@klaire_sawicki)
and Victoria Cumbow (@victoriacumbow)

WRITER: Abby Reuther (@abby.reuther)

SHAKTI POWER YOGA

OVERVIEW: This yoga studio offers a diverse collection of yoga classes, with a focus on Power Yoga.

COST: $$

ADDRESS: 65 Music Square E

NEIGHBORHOOD: Music Row

HOURS: *For the class schedule, please visit their website.*

PHONE: 1.615.942.8100

WEBSITE: shaktiyoganashville.com

INSTAGRAM: @shaktipoweryoga

ATMOSPHERE: Most classes are held in the Shakti Room—an infrared heated room featuring gorgeous historic windows. They also have the unheated Shiva Room upstairs.

HIGHLIGHTS: Sometimes the person to your right is going to be doing a handstand and the person to your left is going to be in child's pose and YOU are welcome to do anything that you feel. Every class is like going to camp: you enter as strangers, you sweat, laugh, and get vulnerable, and you leave having had an experience with friends that you'll never forget!

INSIDER TIPS: Don't be afraid to go for your first time—they'll take good care of you! Sign up for the 30 days for $30.

PHOTOS (LEFT TO RIGHT):
Cristina Dafonte (@cristinadafonte16) and Mary Roberts (@themurnburn)

WRITER: Kate Moore (@moore_kate)

pamper + relax

POPPY & MONROE

OVERVIEW: This natural nail and beauty boutique has services including nails, hair removal, facials, brow and lash, and makeup.

COST: $$

ADDRESS: 604 Monroe St

NEIGHBORHOOD: Germantown

HOURS: Tues – Thur, 11am – 7pm
Fri – Sat, 10am – 7pm

PHONE: 1.615.640.0604

WEBSITE: poppyandmonroe.com

INSTAGRAM: @poppyandmonroe

ATMOSPHERE: It's an old house that has been renovated into a design masterpiece. A bright pink door welcomes you right away, followed by the sweetest staff.

HIGHLIGHTS: Poppy & Monroe use only non-toxic, safe, and environmentally conscious products. They offer waterless services to be as eco-friendly as possible; instead, they use botanical cleansing spray followed by a warm towel wrap.

INSIDER TIPS: The shop and exterior courtyard are perfect for bridal showers, bachelorette parties, girls' night out, and private parties.

PHOTOS (LEFT TO RIGHT):
Gracie Moakler (@graciemoakler)
Christine Kozuch (@ckozuch)

WRITER:
Abby Reuther (@abby.reuther)

BLOWOUT CO.

OVERVIEW: You can get blowouts, up-dos, and makeup—pretty much everything you need to feel absolutely beautiful.

COST: $$

ADDRESS: 700 12th Ave S, Suite 104
For their other locations, please visit the website.

NEIGHBORHOOD: The Gulch

HOURS: Every day. *Call for current hours.*

PHONE: 1.615.244.8243

WEBSITE: blowoutco.com

INSTAGRAM: @blowoutco

ATMOSPHERE: It's clean, bright, welcoming and beautiful. You'll feel relaxed as their staff spoils and pampers you!

HIGHLIGHTS: The Blowout Co. is perfect for special events like a wedding or a red carpet event, which Director of Operations Deidre DeFelice is totally accustomed to. Or you can go in on your self-care day to get an easy and carefree blowout that can last you all week. And did I mention champagne? Yup, sip the bubbly as they make you feel like a total rock star.

INSIDER TIPS: Make an appointment via the app before you go.

PHOTOS (LEFT TO RIGHT):
Deidre DeFelice (@xo.deidre) and Abby Reuther (@abby.reuther)

WRITER: Kate Moore (@moore_kate)

SCOUT'S BARBERSHOP

OVERVIEW: This hip and trendy barbershop and salon with a unique customer experience serves men, women, and kids.

COST: $$

ADDRESS: 904 Main St

NEIGHBORHOOD: East Nashville
For their other location, please visit the website.

HOURS: Mon – Fri, 9am – 9pm
Sat, 9am – 7pm
Sun, noon – 6pm

PHONE: 1.615.982.8345

WEBSITE: scoutsbarbershop.com

INSTAGRAM: @scoutsbarbershop

ATMOSPHERE: When you walk into this trendy barbershop and salon, you'll be treated to a local Barista Parlor coffee or Little Harpeth beer. Grab a seat on a couch, sit back, sip, and relax as you wait for your cut.

HIGHLIGHTS: Scout's is home to Wheat & Co, a men's quality-made apparel and lifestyle shop.

INSIDER TIPS: If you want a cut or style, just walk in or call ahead to get on the list. If you need a straight razor shave or color, call to book in advance.

PHOTOS (LEFT TO RIGHT):
Mali Schneiter (@malikathleen) and Jackie Wall (@jackierwall)

WRITER: Abby Reuther (@abby.reuther)

DANDELION SALON

OVERVIEW: Dandelion Salon is a whimsical salon providing services that include men and women's haircuts, color, blowouts, and bridal and formal styling.

COST: $$

ADDRESS: 1117 Porter Rd

NEIGHBORHOOD: East Nashville

HOURS: Tues, 10am – 6pm
Wed, 11am – 7pm
Thur – Fri, 10am – 6pm
Sat, 10am – 4pm

PHONE: 1.615.953.3234

WEBSITE: dandelionnashville.com

INSTAGRAM: @dandelionnashville

ATMOSPHERE: There's an antique flair with rustic doors as decoration, vintage seating, a gleaming chandelier, and a claw-foot tub for added dimension.

HIGHLIGHTS: With a full range in prices and stylists, you can choose the artiste who best suits your style. Because they use only the top products in the industry, you'll unquestionably leave feeling stunning! Get ready to make some plans because you'll definitely want to show off.

INSIDER TIPS: Their site allows you to book online and check availability of your favorite stylist. Make sure to book in advance because great talent sells out fast!

PHOTOS: Abby Reuther (@abby.reuther)

WRITER: Aubrey Hine (@aubreyhine)

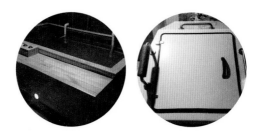

FLOAT NASHVILLE

OVERVIEW: Float Nashville has tanks filled with water and Epsom salt, kept at skin temperature. The salt allows you to float on the surface effortlessly. Leave your stress and pain in the tank and just float away.

COST: $$

ADDRESS: 2701 Greystone Rd

NEIGHBORHOOD: Berry Hill

HOURS: Mon, 5 – 11pm
Tues – Sun, 9am – 11pm

PHONE: 1.615.567.7222

WEBSITE: floatnashville.com

INSTAGRAM: @floatnashville

ATMOSPHERE: It's the most relaxing and stress free atmosphere. Each room and tank is completely private, soundproof, and pitch-black, allowing your body to be free from gravity and outside stimulation.

HIGHLIGHTS: There are numerous benefits from floating: pain relief, injury recovery, muscle soreness, stress relief, and many others.

INSIDER TIPS: If it's your first time floating be sure to check out their FAQs on their website so you're fully prepared for your experience.

Float naked; material against the body can distract from the your sensory experience.

PHOTOS (LEFT TO RIGHT):
Savannah Young (@vannahelayne)
Wendy Nguyen (@Wennnndyy)

WRITER: Abby Reuther (@abby.reuther)

BIOS

ABBY REUTHER

ORIGINALLY FROM: Waupaca, WI

NASHVILLE HAS BEEN HOME FOR: 7 years

LIVE IN: East Nashville

WORK: Founder of *The Nashville Guide*, photographer, and graphic designer

INSTAGRAM: @abby.reuther

FAVORITE NASHVILLE RESTAURANT:
City House and Eastland Cafe

FAVORITE NASHVILLE BUSINESS:
ABEDNEGO and Apple & Oak

A LITTLE MORE ABOUT ME:
I'm a Midwest girl at heart. I love anything outdoors—especially when it involves water. I love supporting local (shocking, right!?). I'll buy anything from a brand that gives back to a great cause. I could watch documentaries all day, every day, and not get bored. I'm a proud aunt. I'm addicted to chocolate and decorating.

MY PERFECT DAY IN NASHVILLE:
Sleep in and snuggle with my pup, Finn. I'd go to Pied Piper for breakfast. Take a long walk at Shelby Park. Stop by Wild Cow for lunch and a fresh juice. Then I'd do a little day drinking downtown and hit up Acme rooftop and The Stage. Then, dinner at City House, ordering the Belly Ham Pizza (obviously). Ice cream afterward from Bobbie's Dairy Dip for dessert. And finally, to top off the perfect day, I would have to end it with puppy snuggles and a little TV.

PHOTO: Michael Reuther (@michaelreuther)

JOE BEECROFT

ORIGINALLY FROM: Ipswich, England

NASHVILLE HAS BEEN HOME FOR: 3 years

LIVE IN: East Nashville

WORK: I am currently developing and starting my own business, The Local Perspective.

INSTAGRAM: @thelocalperspective

FAVORITE NASHVILLE RESTAURANT:
5th & Taylor

FAVORITE NASHVILLE BUSINESS:
Peter Nappi

A LITTLE MORE ABOUT ME:
Originally from England, I'm soccer (real football) obsessed. I play 2 to 3 times a week and still avidly follow my team from back home, rising at 6am most weekends to watch them on TV. A self-described foodie, I love to cook as much as I love to eat out. I'm a beer fanatic and so Nashville has been perfect for me. I spend the majority of my current time developing my business, The Local Perspective.

MY PERFECT DAY IN NASHVILLE:
It would start on the East Side with brunch at Marche and then renting bikes to head downtown. Once there, drinks on the rooftops at Acme, Tootsies, and The Stage, mixing with the tourists. Then I'd bike to Germantown to wander through the shops like Peter Nappi and Wilder before stopping for a late lunch at Little Donkey. Then 5th & Taylor for dinner. If we feel up to it, we would check out No 308 later that evening for dancing.

PHOTO: Ben Lalisan (@benlalisan)

HOLLY DARNELL

ORIGINALLY FROM: Franklin, TN

NASHVILLE HAS BEEN HOME FOR: 6 years

LIVE IN: The Nations

WORK: Registered dietitian and owner of Golden Roots, a thoughtfully hand-picked, local recipe service using Tennessee farms. I also work at Bongo Bakery and work for a personal chef.

INSTAGRAM: @hollywood_25

FAVORITE NASHVILLE RESTAURANT:
Rolf & Daughters

FAVORITE NASHVILLE BUSINESS:
ABEDNEGO

A LITTLE MORE ABOUT ME:
I love cooking for friends and throwing dinner parties. My boyfriend is also a pretty legit cook, so I enjoy being in the kitchen and cooking with him and eating whatever he fixes. I'm also passionate about health and fitness, and enjoy going to the gym and doing yoga. I also love to try new restaurants and go to beer/wine pairing dinners. Basically anything that has to do with food, and I'm there. My family also lives close by and I love spending time with them.

MY PERFECT DAY IN NASHVILLE:
Sleep in a little and go workout at getFIT615. I would go to Riverside Grillshack for a biscuit sandwich. I'd do a little food shopping at the Farmers Market to prepare for dinner with friends at night, then an afternoon pit stop for a hand-dipped cone at Bobbie's Dairy Dip. I'd finish up the day by being surrounded by all of my loves: my boyfriend, friends, and food/wine.

PHOTO: Abby Reuther (@abby.reuther)

KELLEY GRIGGS

ORIGINALLY FROM: Georgetown, KY

NASHVILLE HAS BEEN HOME FOR: 4 years

LIVE IN: East Nashville

WORK: I work with a tech startup called GameWisp, helping streamers and other content creators build subscription services.

INSTAGRAM: @kelleyboothe

FAVORITE NASHVILLE RESTAURANT:
Chauhan Ale & Masala House

FAVORITE NASHVILLE BUSINESS:
It's a toss-up between BookMan/BookWoman and The Belcourt.

A LITTLE MORE ABOUT ME:
I am a writer and graphic designer. Most of the time I'm working on either my day job or my own projects, but in my spare time, I love to practice my creative skills.

MY PERFECT DAY IN NASHVILLE:
I'd walk down to Sky Blue Cafe in the early morning, before it gets too busy. Then I'd bike to either Grimey's or Bookman/BookWoman for a day of book/record hunting. If it's the summer, I'll probably make time for a canoe ride or trip to Percy Priest Lake. Later I'd want to see a show with friends or share a dinner with my husband at home. If it's winter, we usually catch a movie at The Belcourt Theatre (or see an indoor show at the Ryman). Throw in Bobby's Dairy Dip and late night darts at Villager and I'll be out all night.

PHOTO: Megan Sweeting (@bourbonandbrides)

AUBREY HINE

ORIGINALLY FROM: Ashburn, VA

NASHVILLE HAS BEEN HOME FOR: 3 years

LIVE IN: Germantown

WORK: Advertising/Marketing at G/O Digital

INSTAGRAM: @aubreyhine

FAVORITE NASHVILLE RESTAURANT:
Saint Anejo and City House

FAVORITE NASHVILLE BUSINESS:
Emerson Grace

A LITTLE MORE ABOUT ME:
I'm enrolled in ClassPass, allowing me to
try out hundreds of different fitness studios
from boot camps to spin classes to Pilates.
I love finding different ways to stay active
and anything to support local businesses is
always a plus. I've started to make a list of
new (and not so new) restaurants I haven't
been to yet to switch things up a few times
a month. I've recently taken up calligraphy
as well. I swoon over the artists who use this
form of design to create art, gifts, cards, or
simple daily quotes to live by.

MY PERFECT DAY IN NASHVILLE:
I would wake up early, grab some friends and
a few dozen cronuts from Five Daughters
Bakery and set out to the lake and take up
paddle boarding with Nashville Paddle
Company, or spend the day on the water
canoeing with the people I most enjoy
sharing my time with. Nashville has some
of the most beautiful sights to see and I
wouldn't want to be anywhere else.

PHOTO: Marissa Pellegrino (@marissapelle)

ALLISON HOLLEY

ORIGINALLY FROM: We moved often, but I spent the most time in Northern California and Florida.

NASHVILLE HAS BEEN HOME FOR: 6 years

LIVE IN: East Nashville

WORK: I own a little shop called Apple & Oak!

INSTAGRAM: @appleandoaknash

FAVORITE NASHVILLE RESTAURANT:
Mas Tacos and Rolf & Daughters

FAVORITE NASHVILLE BUSINESS:
Well, I'm partial to my little shop! One of my dear friends owns Vinnie Louise, it's a great and affordable women's clothing boutique. I also love Two Old Hippies in The Gulch!

A LITTLE MORE ABOUT ME:
I love to explore Nashville, go out to eat, and drink on porches with my friends. I love to try new places and support local businesses. Social activities keep me going, although on Friday nights, I hide in my bed with my computer, red wine, and my two amazing pups.

MY PERFECT DAY IN NASHVILLE:
First, I'd get a cold brew to go from Barista Parlor and avocado toast from Crema. Then I would spend the day on Broadway with friends, on the rooftops of Acme and The George Jones Museum, and stop by Paradise Park and Robert's. At Robert's, I would eat the yummiest Fried Bologna Sandwich. Then we would head back to our house for a backyard bonfire & a Wii Just Dance costume party.

PHOTO: Rob Norris (@ForRobNorris)

KATE MOORE

ORIGINALLY FROM: Richmond, VA

NASHVILLE HAS BEEN HOME FOR: Since 2007 with a 2-year hiatus, but I couldn't stay away and have been back full time since 2011.

LIVE IN: The Belmont/Hillsboro

WORK: I own, operate, and love getFIT615.

INSTAGRAM: @moore_kate

FAVORITE NASHVILLE RESTAURANT:
Burger Up

FAVORITE NASHVILLE BUSINESS:
Do I have to choose?! getFIT615 and Shakti Power Yoga for sure—it's my home.

A LITTLE MORE ABOUT ME:
I love spending time outside with Emma, getFIT615's mascot and my best friend (@readyforEMMAthing). I also love writing and spending time with friends over coffee and spicy margs. I also love cooking.

MY PERFECT DAY IN NASHVILLE:
I'd start my day teaching a class at getFIT615, then I'd get through my inbox at Steadfast Coffee over an almond milk latte or coffee soda and poached eggs. I'd take Emma on a long hike or maybe paddleboarding, get in some yoga, get in a workout, and then I'd head to the Turnip Truck for some lunch. After that I'd relax at home, maybe write a little bit, check a few more emails. And then I'd have some dinner and spicy margs with a friend or two and go to bed! Get me outside, give me coffee, feed me and let me sweat and I'll stick around forever :)

PHOTO: Lindsey Kanes (@lkanes)

SARAH PATTON

ORIGINALLY FROM: Union City, TN

NASHVILLE HAS BEEN HOME FOR: 12 years

LIVE IN: Green Hills

WORK: Owner of Social Bliss Events and founder of Creative Souls

INSTAGRAM: @sarahcharlottepatton

FAVORITE NASHVILLE RESTAURANT:
Wednesday "Girls Night Out" at Cabana

FAVORITE NASHVILLE BUSINESS:
Bloom Flowers

A LITTLE MORE ABOUT ME:
I love inspiring women to go after their dreams and help them tackle the "crazy" ideas—the ones people tell you are not attainable. Well, they are, and you should always chase your dreams.

I am in love with Nashville and enjoy telling people where to go and what to do in the city. I adore my tribe and family, reading, and traveling. I have a heart for missions, especially to Africa. I love meeting new friends; my motto is "The more the merrier!"

MY PERFECT DAY IN NASHVILLE:
I'd start the day with a morning hike at Radnor Lake, then grab coffee at Frothy Monkey. Next, I'd waltz down the street to Urban Grub for patio time and the best donuts before heading to Centennial Park to catch some local bands at Musician's Corner. Shopping at Blush and The Impeccable Pig for the perfect outfit comes next. Then I'd pamper myself at The Nail Bar in Green Hills and get a blowout at Blow Out Co. before a night on the town with the girls.

PHOTO: Abby Reuther (@abby.reuther)

KRISTEN SHOATES

ORIGINALLY FROM: Raleigh, NC

NASHVILLE HAS BEEN HOME FOR: 5.5 years

LIVE IN: Currently, West End. But as a serial mover, I've lived in Green Hills and Hillsboro Village.

WORK: I work as a strategist and writer for a marketing agency that specializes in working with nonprofits; I freelance write; and I help my husband run our business—Sky Studios, a local music lesson and recording studio.

INSTAGRAM: @kristennicole86

FAVORITE NASHVILLE RESTAURANT:
M.L. Rose, Fido, 12 South Taproom, or Burger Up.

FAVORITE NASHVILLE BUSINESS:
Grimey's and Thistle Farms

A LITTLE MORE ABOUT ME:
I'm a huge fan of music and am often out at shows or browsing record stores. Travel is one of my biggest passions, and I love anything adventurous like hiking and kayaking. I'm also into health and wellness, reading, fashion, art, film, and exploring our amazing city.

MY PERFECT DAY IN NASHVILLE:
First, coffee at Frothy Monkey or another local coffee shop. I'd go for a hike at Percy Warner Park, then spend the afternoon perched up on a patio writing, or wandering through fun neighborhoods like Hillsboro Village or 12 South. I'd have dinner at a local restaurant, with cocktails or a visit to a local brewery, and end the evening listening to records at home.

PHOTO: Abby Reuther (@abby.reuther)

ALEXANDER TAPPER

ORIGINALLY FROM: Nashville, TN

NASHVILLE HAS BEEN HOME FOR:
13 years

LIVE IN: East Nashville

WORK: I started a web design marketplace called Designlive.co—we build websites over screen-share!

INSTAGRAM: @fantasticmrtapp

FAVORITE NASHVILLE RESTAURANT:
Rolf & Daughters

FAVORITE NASHVILLE BUSINESS:
Shakti Yoga and High Garden

A LITTLE MORE ABOUT ME:
I'm a wayward songwriter and jazz junkie. I prefer when things line up at right angles. Since I'm at the computer for work, I try to spend my free time outdoors. I practice yoga daily—inversions are my favorite and I attempt at least one handstand each day. I bike with my black lab mix, Ramsay, on the greenway—he actually pulls me like a sled dog! In a previous life I studied classical guitar, led my college rugby team to an SEC championship, and took 10,000 photos underwater while SCUBA diving.

MY PERFECT DAY IN NASHVILLE:
First, breakfast at Steadfast, then a trip to Rock Island state park for cliff jumping. Next I'd have lunch at Dozen Bakery; front row seats at the Ryman; a late night dinner on the patio at Rolf & Daughters; and a nightcap and dancing at No 308.

PHOTO: Jamie Clayton (@jamieclayton)

APPENDIX

APPENDIX

NEIGHBORHOODS:

DOG-FRIENDLY:

HAPPY HOUR:

KID-FRIENDLY:

TAKES RESERVATIONS/APPOINTMENTS:

PRICE:

NEIGHBORHOOD MAP

ALPHABETICAL INDEX

NOTES